Family and/or Career
Plans of First-Time Mothers

Research in Clinical Psychology, No. 2

Peter E. Nathan, Series Editor

Professor and Chairman
Department of Clinical Psychology
Rutgers, the State University

Other Titles in This Series

Family and/or Career
Plans of First-Time Mothers

by
Debra L. Behrman

UMI RESEARCH PRESS
Ann Arbor, Michigan

Produced and distributed by
UMI Research Press
an imprint of
University Microfilms International
Ann Arbor, Michigan 48106

Library of Congress Cataloging in Publication Data

Behrman, Debra L.
    Family and/or career.

    (Studies in clinical psychology ; no. 2)
    Revision of thesis (Ph.D.)—Northwestern University,
1980.
    Bibliography: p.
    Includes index.
    1. Mother and child—United States. 2. Mothers—Employ-
ment—United States. 3. Pregnant-women—United States—
Attitudes. 4. Husbands—United States—Attitudes.   I. Title.
II. Series.
HQ759.B44 1982   646.7'8   82-17572
ISBN 0-8357-1381-4

Contents

List of Tables

Acknowledgments

I would like to express my sincere gratitude to Dr. Gary Bond, whose availability, guidance and enthusiasm throughout the planning and completion of this work has been invaluable.

I would also like to extend my appreciation to Dr. Larry Feldman and Dr. Frank Summers for their helpful suggestions and interest.

Many thanks are also due to the Lamaze teachers and couples who so willingly cooperated in this project and without whom it would not have been possible.

To my family, special thanks for their continued encouragement and belief in me.

Finally, I thank my husband, Dan, for his patience and help during all stages of this work, and most especially, for his support and love.

1

Introduction

In recent decades, the role of women in American society has undergone fluctuation and critical analysis. With the reemergence of the feminist movement (Chafe, 1977; Humphrey, 1975), decrease in birth rate (Hayghe, 1976; Van Dusen and Sheldon, 1976), increasing acceptance of alternatives to the traditional nuclear family (Bernard, 1972) and other social changes (Nye, 1974), women (as well as men) have begun to examine their place in society and to expand their definition of their proper roles.

There has been a dramatic increase, for example, in the number of women, especially married women, who have entered the labor force (U.S. Department of Commerce, 1979), and women are increasingly viewing paid employment as a source of gratification and identity that was once confined almost exclusively to the roles of wife and mother. At the same time, a growing number of young women are pursuing professional careers that require a great deal of education and commitment (Parrish, 1974). This data suggests an increasing commitment on the part of women, particularly college graduates, to carving out careers and to viewing family life as only one part of their multiple interests (Chafe, 1977).

Despite these changes, there is a great deal of controversy regarding the degree to which women's roles have been, or should be, expanded to simultaneously include that of career woman as well as mother and wife. A particularly current issue involves whether these dual roles may successfully be integrated when there are young children involved.

For today's young women, this issue is bound to activate some degree of role conflict (i.e., antagonism between the requirements of two or more roles). Having been raised during a period when motherhood was "sacred," many, if not most, women have to some extent internalized the view that the responsibility for raising normal, healthy children lies with the mother. Successfully meeting this responsibility has traditionally meant devoting oneself—full-time—to this task. At the same time, recent societal changes have focused attention on this traditional ideology, bringing it under increasing attack. Women have been encouraged to seek higher education and training for professional careers, in preparation to take their rightful places in society as individuals who are as capable as men to function successfully and to make meaningful contributions outside the domestic sphere.

These changes have brought about many opportunities for women but have also raised questions and conflicts in regard to individual choices surrounding motherhood and employment, conflicts that seem to be particularly activated at the point of the first pregnancy. Before this time, successfully combining marriage and a career presents fewer complications and difficulties. When contemporary women are about to enter the stage of motherhood, though, they must deal with often conflicting pressures from society, family and themselves. Having made the decision to become a mother, a woman must then consider her current feelings and future plans regarding her role as mother-wife and her role as employee-career person. She must choose whether to continue working, combining a career with motherhood, or to focus all her energies on her family, temporarily or permanently ending her career. (Although it may be said that a parallel choice faces men, the reality of men's roles in today's society does not support this. The vast majority of American men expect to continue full-time employment during their adult lives. In fact, there is evidence that most men increase their career commitment when they begin fatherhood [Safilios-Rothschild, 1976].)

This decision has numerous social and personal ramifications for all involved and is the subject of this paper. Despite past research that has focused on the working mother's attitudes, personality and motivations for employment, it is unclear why some women combine dual roles while others focus on either a career or, more often, a family. In particular, there has been little investigation of how women choosing opposite alternatives differ at the point at which they make their plans. For those women who want children (still true of the vast majority), this point would seem to occur during the first pregnancy.

The present study then will investigate factors that may be associated with a woman's plans to interrupt or continue her career at the birth of her first child. It is expected that, as a byproduct, this investigation will further our understanding of the degree to which changing societal forces have had an impact on contemporary women. If society is to benefit from their many talents and if women themselves are to truly be able to have and enjoy expanding options, it is important that we discover those factors that act to encourage or inhibit individuals from realizing their potential and taking full advantage of promising sources of personal fulfillment.

2

Literature Review

Participation of Women in the Labor Force

Labor force participation by women has changed dramatically in the past two decades. This is nowhere more evident than in statistics indicating the employment status of women with young children. Working women, and working mothers, are no longer considered a rarity; rather, they are a growing force with substantial impact on American society and its economy.

In this section, a brief historical perspective on working women in America will be presented, followed by a more detailed examination of the characteristics of working women and their families.

Historical Perspective

Despite the fact that the working woman in the United States is considered to be a relatively new phenomenon, women have always played an important part in the American economy and its industrial development. Certainly women have always worked to produce goods for their families—food, clothing and household items—and often for sale to others. While it is true that the majority of women in early American society worked in the home, a small proportion did earn money in trades and industries, and by operating schools, taverns or shops. A 1789 petition for the first cotton factory in Massachusetts, stating that it would "afford employment to a great number of women and children, many of whom will be otherwise useless, if not burdensome to society" (Nye, 1974, p. 2), is just one example of the fact that working women were not always considered negatively. In fact, support for such work was based not only on economic reasons but on moral factors as well. It was argued that women employees would otherwise become idle, engage in "vices" and become a burden to society. In 1850, the first manufacturing census showed employment of almost one million persons, 24 percent of whom were women (Nye, 1974).

In the nineteenth and early twentieth centuries, the industrial revolution gained increasing momentum. Much of the work that had previously been performed in the home (like making cloth or soap) was transferred to factories, and the number of women in paid employment, though small, began to rise. By 1910, women constituted 21 percent of the entire labor force, and by 1940, 25 percent (Nye, 1974).

Although economic, social and technical changes that would have a major impact on the employment of women were occurring rapidly, their effect was not really felt until World War II. During the depression of the 1930s, women, and in particular, married women, were consciously discouraged from working and, until the war, a surplus of labor made employment opportunities meager.

The situation changed drastically during World War II, however, as women were urged to enter the labor force in large numbers, to take over for the men serving in the armed forces and to meet the demands for war production. After the war, a large proportion of these women returned home, but the stage was set. The expansion of the American economy after the war, a shortage of labor, and the increased demand for workers in fields that were traditionally female—teaching, nursing and service occupations— all contributed to a growth in the number of working women. In 1940, 27.4 percent of the female population were employed; in 1960, 34.8 percent; and in 1979, 50.8 percent. Over 40 percent of the entire labor force is now composed of women (U.S. Dept. of Commerce, 1979).

Changes in the Family Characteristics of Working Women

The increase in the number of employed women during the past decades is largely accounted for by the increased participation of new groups of women. Prior to 1940, the majority of working women were single. In 1900, for example, only 15 percent of all employed women were married and they constituted only 3 percent of the entire labor force (Nye, 1974). Looking at it another way, in 1900 only 5.6 percent of married women were working; by 1940 this had increased only to about 15 percent (Hayghe, 1976). In contrast, by 1979, 49 percent of married women in the United States were employed (Johnson, 1980).

These married women entered the labor force at different rates and at different times depending on their family situation. By the 1950s, it was common for women to work after they were married but only until the birth of their first child. In the early 1950s, older women whose children were presumably grown began to enter the labor force in greater numbers, showing the largest increases in employment rates of married women (Hayghe, 1976). There were a number of factors that contributed to this. Continued economic developments had increased the demand for labor, including female labor, but the supply of those women who were typically in the labor force could not meet the demand. In fact, there was an absolute, as well as relative, decrease in the number of single women available (Oppenheimer, 1973) due to a decline in the birth rate in the 1930s and early 1940s. Further, women began marrying at earlier ages. For example, by 1950, 49 percent of the women had married by age 20 compared to only 35 percent ten years earlier (Nye, 1974). Since many of these women had children within a year or two, they quickly left the labor force. The increase in birth rates during the early 1950s contributed to the sustained removal of these young women from the ranks of the employed. Thus, there was an increased opportunity for older women to return to work.

Demand for women workers, in particular, continued to rise as the need for white-collar workers grew. These occupations required little physical strength and many positions were staffed primarily by women. Secretarial, nursing, teaching and many service occupations were felt to be particularly suitable for women; in addition, men were often not attracted to these jobs because of the comparatively low pay.

At the same time, the demands on married women were being reduced. Household tasks had become less time-consuming as technology rapidly advanced. Childcare too demanded less time from women as birth rates again began to fall after 1955. In addition, childbearing became concentrated in the few years following marriage. The youngest child often began school before his or her mother had reached her middle thirties.

Thus, in the late 1950s and early 1960s these economic and sociological changes began to bring married women with dependent children into the labor force in ever-increasing numbers. In 1950, 28 percent of women with school-age children only were employed. By 1965, this number had increased by one-half to over 42 percent. Between 1965 and 1978, the rate of increase had slowed to about 30 percent, bringing the number of married employed women with school-age children to 59 percent (Johnson, 1980). (The number is considerably higher for divorced women with school-age children—83.4 percent of these women work.)

In more recent years, a dramatic increase in the participation rates of mothers with preschool children has occurred. In 1950, 12 percent of married women with children under six were in the labor force; in 1960, 18.6 percent; and in 1970, 30.3 percent. By 1979, 43% of married women (with husbands present) who had children under six were employed. (The number increases to 68.9 percent for divorced women.) (Johnson, 1980). A crucial factor behind this shift has been the change in the economy. The onset of the highest inflation to date in this century (Hayghe, 1976) has put increased pressure on families to earn two incomes. Social changes, including lowered birth rates, the Women's Liberation movement, and increased divorce rates, have also contributed to this increase, as has the increased educational level and the number of women entering the professions (Parrish, 1974).

Mothers with Preschool Children

Despite this rapid change, we have not reached the point where most women work outside the home during their childbearing and childrearing years. Currently, 43 percent of married women with children under six and husbands present are employed at some time during the year (Johnson, 1980). However, this rate fluctuates depending on several factors. For example, black women are considerably more likely to be in the labor force than their white counterparts; 62 percent of black women with children under six are employed, while the comparable rate for white women is only 39.7 percent (U.S. Dept. of Commerce, 1979).

Other variables, including age of child, educational level and husband's income, also influence not only employment rates but the degree of participation in the labor force as well. Unless otherwise stated, the following data will consider the effects of these factors for white married women with children under six whose husbands are present. The data was obtained from the U.S. Department of Commerce and applies to the 1978 year.

The age of the child is, of course, an important consideration. The older the child, the more likely the mother is to work. For example, with children between the ages of 14 and 17, 57 percent of mothers were employed; with children between 6 and 13 years, 55.7 percent were employed. The 1978 rate for mothers with children under six, however, was only 39.7 percent; this was reduced further to 35.8 percent when there was a child under three. Of these employed women, 62 percent worked full-time, the others part-time. (The ratio of full-time to part-time workers increases only minimally if the child is older.) That is, only 20 percent of mothers with children under three were working full-time at the time this information was collected.

If we further examine the data regarding degree of participation, we find that 48.9 percent of women with children under three reported working at some time during 1977. However, only 9 percent worked full-time for the entire year. Another 9 percent worked full-time for anywhere from 27 to 49 weeks with 11 percent working full-time for less than 26 weeks. Eight percent of the women reported working part-time for the major part of the year with another 10 percent working part-time for less than half a year. Thus, while the participation rate for mothers with young children appears quite high at first, upon closer examination it becomes clear that only a small percentage actually sustain a full-time work involvement.

The husband's income level is also a relevant factor. Generally, wives' participation rates decrease as husbands' incomes rise. For all women (including nonwhite) between the ages of 25 and 34 with children under six, the participation rate in 1978 was 43 percent. When the husband's income was between $10,000 and $15,000 per year, the rate increased to about 52 percent. Thereafter, the rate rapidly decreased. When the husband's income was between $25,000 and $35,000, the participation rate was only 25 percent. Thereafter the rate remained relatively steady, with only a slight increase to 26 percent where the husband's income was over $50,000.

The relation of income to degree of participation is not reported for women with young children. However, looking at statistics for women with dependent children (under 18), it is apparent that as the husband's income rises, the wife's extent of participation decreases. For example, with husband's income between $15,000 and $19,000, 33 percent of all women employed at some time during the year worked full-time during the entire year; when income rises to over $50,000, this level drops to only 23 percent.

Another relevant variable is the woman's education. For all women with children under six, participation rates generally increased with educational level. Of the women with less than a high school diploma, 36 percent were employed. This rose to 40 percent with the completion of high school and 45 percent with some college education. Forty-seven percent of college graduates were in the labor force, increasing to 58 percent for those with more than 16 years of formal education.

If data is examined for both education and husband's income combined, an interesting pattern emerges. For those with 16 years of education or less, the participation rate decreases as husband's income rises. This is not the case, however, for women with some graduate training. Although data is not available for all income levels (due to bases which are too low), it appears that the rate for these women remains relatively constant, if not increasing somewhat, as husband's income rises.

Another apparent trend involves the different rate of decrease depending on educational level as the child's age decreases. In other words, it appears that while well-educated women have moved into the labor force faster than those with little education, in general the differences between groups are less for women with young children. This is especially true for women whose husbands' incomes are in the middle level. For example, for those in the $15,000 to $20,000 range with school-age children, there is a 23-point difference in participation rates between those women with some college education and those at the graduate school level. When these groups of women have children under six, the difference drops to only 12 points. As Nye (1974) suggests, "the inhibiting effects of the childcare role are greater for highly educated women . . . . Thus, the presence of preschool children has reduced the flow of well-educated, energetic young women into the labor force and very young children reduce it even more than do older pre-schoolers" (pp. 15, 18).

Summary

Clearly, there has been a substantial increase since World War II in the number of mothers who combine work and family roles. This is true even for women with very young children. However, despite the amount of attention being given to this phenomenon in the media and academic circles, we are far from the point where mothers of infants and preschoolers have made a substantial commitment to the labor force. While over 40 percent of this group work at some point during the year, less than 10 percent are employed full-time for the entire year (compared to over 70 percent of men) (U.S. Dept. of Commerce, 1979).

Educational and income levels are important mediating factors to be considered. In general, the more education a woman has, the more likely she will be to enter the labor force. The more income her husband earns, the less chance there is that she will work. However, the combination of these factors has varying effects. Women with at least a college education have a relatively high participation rate when there are no preschool children; when young children are present, the rate drops sharply if the husband's income is adequate. For women with lower levels of education the decrease is not as sharp since the base rate is lower.

It would appear then that for those women with only a moderate level of education, participation in the labor force is dependent particularly on the husband's income. If the family income is relatively high, participation rates are relatively low regardless of the age of the children. For women with high levels of education, however, participation seems to be more dependent on the child's age. It would appear that when the youngest child reaches school-age a high percentage of these women return to work even when the family income is substantial.

Thus, different motivating factors seem to be operating for different groups of women, although for all groups the presence of young children acts as a strong deterrent to the dual role involvement of women.

Social Views

As changes in the composition of the labor force have occurred, the issue of the "proper" role of women in contemporary society has become a focus of study and controversy. At one end is the "traditional" view of women as primarily, if not exclusively, mothers and wives; at the other, the "modern" or "feminist" view calls for the complete abolishment of all gender-typed roles. (While these labels will be used throughout this study, they are for purposes of identification only and are not meant to imply a positive or negative judgment on the part of the author.) Investigations of the attitudes of the general population and particular subgroups (especially college students) regarding these issues have reported varying results, as values and behavioral expectations of women have been in a state of flux. In general, however, there has been a shift toward an increased acceptance of expanding sex roles, although attitudes regarding the primary function of women as mothers have been more resistant to change.

The following sections trace the development of these changing ideologies, describing contrasting views in greater detail and reviewing studies pertaining to attitudes toward women's roles.

Traditional View of Sex Roles

In preindustrial times, men and women generally shared the work of providing for the family. With industrialization, however, roles shifted and our society evolved a general pattern of division of labor between home and work, characterized by the assignment of work to men and homemaking to women. A woman's place was held to be in the home, caring for her husband and children and as far removed from the workplace as possible (although, as noted previously, this did not always occur). This pattern was felt to be a reflection of what was right and good: right because it reflected the male's natural superiority and protected the weaker female, good because it insured the well-being of the family (Rapoport and Rapoport, 1978).

In the first half of the twentieth century, this pattern was seen as being interrupted only during the two world wars when large numbers of women entered the labor force. This was considered an extraordinary circumstance and did not alter the social structure and the prevailing notion of proper social roles. When the men returned from the war, the women left their jobs and returned home, at least those women from the middle class.

By the end of World War II, however, there had been many changes in the nature of the tasks women performed. Housework had become simplified with the introduction of many labor-saving devices, fewer children were born, and schools had taken over a large part of their education. Rose (1951) suggests that while men acquired new civic functions with the industrial revolution, women's functions were gradually reduced and many were lost. Because these losses were so gradual, most women did not realize they were occurring and thus did not plan for changes. Further, there was much more opposition to women acquiring new roles, as compared to men, even by a significant number of the women themselves. Rose thus concludes that women's roles were relatively unclear and much less specific than men's.

Despite these changes, the conventional pattern continued, with the assumption that the only significant role for women was in the home. In fact, perhaps because of the reality of these changes, there was a renewed emphasis after World War II on the traditional family pattern. Rossi (1972) notes that "the late 1940's and the 1950's were marked by a national mood of domesticity demonstrated by the rapid rise in the birth rate and the flight of families to the suburbs. It was a period of high praise for women's domestic role" (p. 141).

This traditional view of sex roles encompasses several assumptions, including the superiority of men, and sex-role stereotypes of women as less independent, rational, and ambitious and more passive, emotional and submissive (Broverman, Vogel, Broverman, Clarkson and Rosenkrantz, 1972). However, perhaps the most pervasive set of assumptions underlying this view (and certainly the most relevant to this research) pertains to the belief that motherhood is central to the definition of an adult female. Russo (1976) refers to this as the "motherhood mandate," requiring women to have at least two children and to raise them well. There are two sets of beliefs that are basic to this traditional ideology. The first involves the child's needs; the second, the needs of the woman.

The motherhood mandate asserts that the major responsibility for raising a normal, healthy child rests with the mother. Historically based on biology, this doctrine has continued to be enforced by social and cultural institutions. "Behavioral scientists and clinicians, such as psychiatrists and pediatricians, encouraged acceptance of the model in which the biological mother must provide the major portion of the stimulation, conditioning, and emotional satisfaction deemed essential for normal development of the child" (Wortis, 1971, p. 733).

Psychological studies of attachment behavior and deprivation, for example, have been used to support this assumption. Bowlby (1969) defined and elaborated on the "attachment function," a process in which the infant develops a strong psychobiological need to maintain proximity with the mother and vice versa. The theory assumes a propensity by the mother and infant to develop attachment toward each other and has been interpreted as support for the primacy of the mother-infant relationship (Wortis, 1971). Despite criticisms by other investigators (Schaffer and Emerson, 1964; Spelke, Zelazo, Kagan and Kotelchuck, 1973) who argued that it is erroneous to conclude that an infant must be attached to only one object (the mother) or that all other attachments are secondary, the necessity of an exclusive, or at least primary, mother-infant bond was presumed. This was considered as support for the notion that the mother is biologically the most capable person of raising a child.

A second group of studies (Spitz, 1946) investigated the effects of mother-child separation. Although most of these studies were based on institutionalized children, the suggested deleterious effects of any separation between mother and child is one of the principal arguments used to encourage women to devote their constant attention to infants (Wortis, 1971). As Margaret Mead (1954) wrote:

> At present, the specific biological situation of the continuing relationship of the child to its biological mother and its need for care by human beings are being hopelessly confused in the growing insistence that child and biological mother, or mother surrogate, must never be separated, that all separation even for a few days is inevitably damaging, and that if long enough it does irreversible damage. This . . . is a new and subtle form of antifeminism in which men—under the guise of exalting the importance of maternity—are tying women more tightly to their children than has been thought necessary since the invention of bottle feeding and baby carriages. Actually, anthropological evidence gives no support at present to the value of such an accentuation of the tie between mother and child. On the contrary, cross-cultural studies suggest that adjustment is most facilitated if the child is cared for by many warm, friendly people. . . . It may well be, of course, that limiting a child's contacts to its biological mother may be the most efficient way to produce a character suited to lifelong monogamous marriage, but if so then we should be clear that that is what we are doing, that the biological mother is necessary for a sort of "imprinting" strong enough for monogamy, and that that is the reason we insist that mothers alone care for their children without help from fathers, grandparents, servants, or siblings. [P. 477]

Thus, despite claims that there is no evidence to support such assumptions, it has been widely believed in American society that infants require their mother's undivided attention. Therefore, employment of women has been thought to be incompatible with adequate mothering.

These tenets are a cornerstone of the traditional view of sex roles and a basic justification for the division of labor. As Lorber (1975), a sociologist, asks, "if we remove the structural underpinnings of marriage and the family that have supported these systems in the past—sexual division of labor, economic dependence on males of women and children and the combination of procreation with sex—can we still achieve an orderly system of coupling and childbearing?" (pp. 465-66).

The second set of beliefs underlying the motherhood mandate concerns the mother herself and asserts that a woman's fulfillment is primarily through motherhood; that is, the major goal of a woman's life is to raise well-adjusted children (Russo, 1976). Women have a biological instinct to mother and denial of this is considered to be based on psychological maladjustment (Brazelton, 1969; Greenbaum, 1973; Zambrana, Hurst and Hite, 1979).

One relevant corollary to this doctrine is that women with a strong career interest are viewed with some suspicion. Several investigators, for instance, have suggested that women with career aspirations are rare and maladjusted, rejecting their femininity (Lewis, 1968; McArthur, 1958):

> The girl who aims for a career is likely to be frustrated and dissatisfied with herself as a person. . . . [She is] less well adjusted than those who are content to become housewives. Not only is [she] likely to have a poor self-concept, but she also probably lacks a close relationship with her family. . . . possibility that a career orientation among girls grows out of personal dissatisfaction, so that the career becomes a frustration outlet. [Lewis, 1968, pp. 33-34]

While the traditional ideology described above was perhaps most prevalent in the 1950s and early 60s, its basic assumptions have led to deep-rooted norms that are still espoused today, although perhaps modified to some extent. Helson (1972), for example, states that while investigators are more accepting of the idea that some women have needs and interests outside of the home, they assume that the mother-wife role still has priority. And Zambrana, Hurst and Hite (1979), in a review of literature on the working mother, note that the cultural expectation that the mother's role be exclusive is frequently reinforced, especially in popular childrearing books. They identify several themes found in this literature:

> First, maternal employment during the first years of the child's life is viewed negatively. . . . Further, the mother who works out of choice and not necessity . . . is considered not only to have failed her child but also herself. . . . Second, there is a general consensus that the mother—if she must work—work part-time. . . . Third, there is the implicit, and sometimes overt assumption that the mother is the primary caretaker and only she can assume responsibility of the child. . . . A fourth theme is that a woman with young children is a mother first, and her desire to work should be compromised in each instance, and sacrificed when necessary, to her child. [P. 863]

Thus, the traditional view of sex-roles, far from being an outdated ideology, is quite prominent today. As Wortis (1971) notes, "we all have a strong prejudice about the need for 'mothering' because we were all mothered" (p. 734).

Nontraditional View of Sex Roles

The 1960s saw the emergence of a new ideology based not on the division of labor by gender but on equality between the sexes in all spheres. While traditional orientations stress that a woman's primary goal is to bear and raise healthy children, modern or feminist orientations advocate encouraging women to develop their talents and pursue careers, sharing financial and domestic responsibilities equally with men.

The growth of this new ideology cannot be attributed to a single cause but was the result of "a constellation of social and economic forces [that] had come together, each reinforcing the others, to create a total pattern" (Chafe, 1977, p. 145). Mason, Czajka and Arber (1976) hypothesize that the perceived benefits of the traditional division of labor no longer outweighed the costs. As female wage levels rose, there was the increasing cost of women remaining at home. The decreasing birthrate meant there were fewer years when a total investment in the home was necessary. The rising level of education and the increased number of women who, through divorce, became heads of households, were additional factors. Further, it became more apparent that increasing numbers of women were in the labor force and working women were no longer seen as totally deviant. Up until this time, it seemed that the working woman was "one of America's best kept secrets" (Keller, 1972). Now, social definitions of women's roles were apparently beginning to catch up to reality.

The reemergence of the women's movement was an additional force, exposing American society to a new ideology and disseminating information that questioned the traditional norms. The current movement is often said to have begun with the publication of *The Feminine Mystique* (1963) in which Friedan scrutinized the post-World War II rise of domesticity and concluded that the picture of the American woman as a fulfilled and happy housewife was a myth.

The problems engendered by the traditional view of women's roles were addressed even before Friedan, however. Komarovsky, for example, in 1946, hypothesized that women face conflicting, if not mutually exclusive, expectations. Interviews with female college seniors revealed that many were suffering from confusion and anxiety regarding appropriate sex role behaviors. While these women were raised with pressures to excel intellectually when younger, they were quite suddenly given contrasting messages and expected to conform to the more traditional feminine roles as adults.

This view has continued to be espoused by supporters of the feminist viewpoint. It is believed that antagonism between female needs and desires and the behaviors expected of them have resulted in conflict and frustration for a great many women today (Clavan, 1970; Seiden, 1976; Westervelt, 1973). Proponents of this view cite research showing that marriage and childrearing are associated for women with less happiness, more stress and more overt mental illness (Dohrenwend and Dohrenwend, 1974; Huber, 1973; Powell and Reznikoff, 1976), concluding that this is the result of the conflict between personal needs and cultural role expectations.

While aspects of the feminist ideology, such as equal pay for equal work, seem to have gained wide support, other aspects, especially views concerning the family, have remained more controversial. There is concern, for instance, that feminists favor the abolishment of the conjugal family system, viewing it as the basis of their oppression and that they will "exchange one set of prescribed and proscribed behaviors for another" (Clavan, 1970, p. 322).

Studies of Sex-Role Attitudes

Studies undertaken in the 1950s and early 1960s reported that most men and women held traditional views of the appropriate roles for women (Astin and Nichols, 1964; Davis and Oleson, 1965; Siegal and Haas, 1963). Only a small percentage approved of women combining maternal and work roles, especially if for other than financial reasons.

Glenn (1959) assessed the attitudes of 250 white women, with a range of educational backgrounds, from a small southern community. One-third of the women were employed themselves. He asked his subjects to indicate whether they approved of women working under a variety of conditions, including varying ages of children and different motivations. While a majority favored childless women working, approval decreased when there were children present, correlating with the age of the child (i.e., approval decreased if the child was younger). The stated reason for working was an important factor. For example, 87 percent approved of a mother of a preschooler working if she was working for the "necessities of life"; however, only 17 percent approved of her working because "homemaking didn't keep her interested" and only 15 percent endorsed employment if it was because "her education is wasted if she doesn't work." Age, education and socio-economic status of the respondents were not significant. Glenn concluded that there was a strong norm against working mothers, especially if they had preschool children, that cut across all socioeconomic status lines.

Studies of the future plans of female college students affirmed the then prevalent norm of women's roles as being predominantly in the home. Rose (1951) questioned male and female students regarding expectations about their adult roles. The women students desired an average of 3.6 children and expected to spend the majority of their waking hours in household tasks. While as many women as men expected to seek a job after graduation, 28 percent to 39 percent of these women (depending on socioeconomic level) expected to retire permanently from all paid employment before the age of 30. (None of the men had similar expectations.) These women then not only did not expect to work when caring for children, but had made no provisions for returning to work even after the children were grown and household responsibilities were no longer as time-consuming.

A study of attitudes of entering freshmen at the University of Minnesota was reported by Hewer and Neubeck (1964). They administered a questionnaire tapping beliefs about working women to the freshman class of 1959.

The results indicate that the students, in general, believed that a woman could fulfill herself, her abilities, and her interests in the home. The majority did not accept a woman working because "housework provides inadequate opportunity for the expression of intellectual interests," "insufficient challenge," or "to make use of their abilities." They approved of women working to "meet financial responsibilities," "to buy extra things for home and family," and "to help their husbands complete their education." Over 90 percent disapproved of women working when there were preschool children. The authors concluded the majority of these students "accept the traditional and nurturant role for women. . . . There is little evidence of a cultural change. In fact, there may be a denial of it. The majority of these women believe their place is in the home. They seem to want it that way and agree to venture out only when they can earn money to increase the comfort and well-being of their families" (p. 591).

As the sixties and seventies progressed, however, dual roles for women became commonplace and many studies indicated that the idea of a woman having both a career and a family had become not only more acceptable but even desirable (Almquist and Angrist, 1970; Poloma, 1972).

A 1974 Roper Poll (Cummings, 1977) reported that over half of the women questioned favored combining marriage, children and a career. Forty-five percent of 18 to 24 year old women chose such a combination as the most satisfying type of life in a 1975 Gallup poll (Cummings, 1977), and a 1980 Roper Poll of American women revealed that "many intend to have both full-time careers and families and see no conflict in maintaining both" (Carmichael, 1980).

Steinmann (1974), in research extending over twenty years, investigated where women in general place themselves in regard to the traditional and liberal concepts of the feminine role. She defined the traditional concept as one in which the woman is the "other," fulfilling herself by meeting the needs of her husband and children, while according to the liberal concept, the woman fulfills herself through her own self-achievements. In a review of this research, Steinmann concluded that "all over the world, the same pattern emerged, a pattern that showed little variation among different age groups, ethnic groups and educational groups . . . . Women universally share a desire to combine self-realization (outside the home) with the more traditional nurturant rules bestowed on them" (p.54). Furthermore, although these subjects believed that men preferred women who were strongly family-oriented, there was almost no difference between men's reported ideal woman and the women's reported ideal woman or their own self-perceptions.

Yorburg and Arafat (1975) surveyed over one thousand men and women in New York City in an attempt to assess current sex-role conceptions. They found that the majority of both men and women opted for more equality between the sexes, less arbitrary sex-typing and less role segregation at work and in the family, although the women in this sample were significantly less traditional than the men. In the question perhaps most pertinent to this review ("Do you advocate the dual role of today's women in the home and in the economy?"), 80 percent of the males and 89.9 percent of the females responded favorably.

Research pertaining to college students' attitudes toward the role of women and their future expectations of themselves or their wives in this regard confirms that a majority currently advocate both family and occupational roles for women. Almquist (1974), for example, found that over 60 percent of a group of undergraduates had generally favorable attitudes toward working wives and Bayer (1975) reported that less than 20 percent of female college freshmen thought that "the activities of married women are best confined to the home and family."

Walker and Walker (1977), using the semantic differential technique, asked university students to rate the concept "working mother with pre-school children." They found that this concept was judged as socially acceptable, liberal-assertive and tense and concluded that there was a generally favorable evaluative component to this idea.

When asked about their own plans, many of the women responded in terms of a combination of roles. A study of lower middle-class college women (Epstein and Bronzaft, 1972) reports that a plurality of 48 percent expected that in fifteen years they would be "married career women with children," while only 28 percent saw themselves as "housewives with one or more children." Rand and Miller (1972) questioned a cross-section of college women and found that 35 percent expected to work most of the time and an additional 20 percent planned to return to work once their children were in school. Cummings (1977) reports that the combination of marriage, family and career was seen as a "very rewarding" way to live by over two-thirds of the women in her sample, and 85 percent expected to attain this goal.

While it would be difficult to compare such data with that of earlier studies due to different populations and research methods, several investigators have attempted to analyze comparable data over time. Parelius (1975) sampled female college students in 1969 and 1973 utilizing identical questionnaires that assessed general orientations toward women and work as well as expectations regarding their own roles. A greater percentage of women in 1973 strongly agreed that women are as competent as men in any job (79 percent versus 61 percent in 1969). In terms of their own plans, 63 percent of the women (as compared to 56 percent in 1969) intended to combine marriage, family and a career. While in 1969, 52 percent advocated interrupting their careers until their children were grown, only 37 percent endorsed this plan in 1973. Conversely, 37 percent in 1973 intended to keep working their entire adult lives while only 16 percent had this expectation in

1969. Thus there was a clear shift in these women's general attitudes toward sexual equality, and in their own plans and expectations, although they were more committed to such equality in the abstract than in their own lives.

In another comparative study, Roper and Labeff (1977) contrasted data from a 1934 study of sex-role attitudes with a similar questionnaire administered in 1974. Questionnaires in both studies were given to students and their parents and yielded feminism scores on scales tapping economic, domestic, political and conduct issues. While specific items were not presented, the authors reported that there was a general trend toward more egalitarian attitudes in all spheres for both students and parents. Both generations, however, were more favorable concerning equal status in the political and economic spheres compared to domestic and conduct concerns.

Thus, research to date confirms that there has been an increasing change over the years toward a more modern ideology in both the college and general populations, including majority acceptance of dual roles for women and the expectation by many women that they will combine work and family roles.

There is some indication, however, that these attitudinal changes have reached their peak. Astle (1979), for instance, in a study comparing the 1972, 1974 and 1977 National Opinion Research Center General Social Surveys concludes that "all variables analyzed across time have shown a move toward traditionalism from 1974 to 1977" (p. 5152).

Certainly, attitudes toward the primary role of women as mothers have not changed as dramatically, especially when considering mothers of small children. In a *McCall's* magazine poll (Greenbaum, 1973), 76 percent of the 20,000 women who responded, regardless of age or education, felt that young children need a full-time mother. When married, currently or recently employed Detroit women between the ages of 18 and 44 were questioned, 69 percent responded that "a working mother can establish just as warm and secure a relationship with her children as a mother who does not work"; however, over one-half felt that "a preschool child is likely to suffer if his mother works" (Mason, Czajka and Arber, 1976).

This norm, still prevalent in our society, which prescribes full-time care of young children by their mothers is reflected in the future plans of women students and the expectations of their male counterparts. Farley (1969) reports that only 27 percent of female graduate students who said that their careers were very important to them planned to work full-time when they had preschool children. Other studies (Cummings, 1977; Edwards, 1969; Komarovsky, 1973; Rand and Miller, 1972) also report that the majority of women (the number varies depending on other variables such as type of career and sex role attitudes) plan to remain home at least while their children are small.

Almquist (1974) asked female students at a southwestern university to indicate whether they would personally want to be employed under a variety of conditions, male students whether they would want their wives working. The average response was 70 percent (64 percent for men) who definitely or probably would want to work. However, there was considerable variation depending on the conditions. The author reported that most women envisioned themselves working in the "establishing" phase—before there were children—to help earn money, to put their husbands through graduate school, etc. In other words, their role was a supportive one. Almost none of these students (only 9 percent) wanted to work during the next family stage—when there were preschool children. The male students responded similarly. In McMillan's (1972) study, only 4 percent of the male students preferred their future wives to have continuous work involvement.

Komarovsky (1973) interviewed male students regarding their role expectations, preferences and limits of tolerance. The majority valued competence, resourcefulness and intelligence in women and, in response to structured questions, had favorable attitudes toward working wives. Further probing, however, revealed conflicting attitudes. She eventually classified the men into four groups. Twenty-four percent were considered traditionalists, intending to marry women who would remain in the home. Seven percent were at the other end: these "feminist" types were willing to significantly change their own roles to facilitate the woman's career. Sixteen percent were particularly conflicted about this issue, abstractly favoring their future wives working but putting unrealistic and demanding qualifications on their approval. Almost half (the "modified traditionalists") favored their wives quitting work to raise their children, then returning once they were grown. The author concludes that "attitudes toward working wives abounded in ambivalences and inconsistencies. The ideological supports for the traditional sex role differentiation in marriage are weakening, but the emotional allegiance to the modified traditional pattern is still strong" (p. 884).

In part, this seems a reflection of the view that a woman's primary responsibility is to her family and that any career interest should be secondary. Steinmann and Fox (1970) note that students in their sample generally agreed that "marriage and children should come first in a woman's life" and that "a woman's main interest is to raise normal, well-behaved children." Parelius (1975) reports that although 60 percent of the women in her study expected to work most of their adult lives, and 80 percent believed that a wife's career is equal in importance to her husband's, only a small minority would sacrifice marriage or motherhood for occupational success. Over half of the Detroit women in Mason, Czajka and Arber's study (1976) agreed that "it is much better for everyone involved if the man is the achiever outside the home and the woman takes care of the home and family," and Garland (1972) noted that the men in his study, while generally having positive attitudes toward their wives' work, saw a career as being second in importance to their wives' domestic roles.

The belief that working women are not able to adequately meet their home responsibilities is also a factor. Studies of married professionals, for instance, indicate that the men especially are likely to believe that professional women cannot adequately fulfill both home and career obligations and will not be able to meet their responsibilities to their children and husbands as successfully as the full-time homemaker (Etaugh, 1973; Kaley, 1971).

The attitude that a woman achieves fulfillment by being a successful mother and wife is also visible. For instance, in a sample of female college graduates, in response to a question regarding the type of success these women would most like to achieve, the most frequent responses were to be the mother of several accomplished children and to be the wife of a prominent man (Rossi, 1972).

Certainly, all Americans do not agree with this. Rosen (1974), for instance, found that female medical students adamantly rejected the view that motherhood was an essential and central part of the female role. While the male students were somewhat more oriented toward a traditional role for women, they too felt that childrearing was not necessary for a woman's fulfillment and few felt that women belong exclusively in the home. Even among this group of students, however, only 8 percent felt that a woman should give her career priority over motherhood.

Summary

There has been a great deal of controversy recently concerning the extent to which attitudinal and behavioral changes have occurred in the area of women's roles. Studies are often inconsistent and data dependent on the investigator's interpretation. Depending on the focus of the research, one could as easily conclude that few women and men accept true equality and non-sex-typing of roles as that there has been a dramatic turning away from traditional ideology.

Certainly the literature regarding attitudes and expectations towards women's sex roles supports the hypothesis that there has been a change in the conceptualization of these roles, especially during the past 10 to 15 years. Support for sexual equality, in general, has increased, although this support has been somewhat less in the family sphere than in the political or economic areas.

Furthermore, there is now basic recognition of the fact that a great many women do work and an acceptance of their dual roles. A woman's place is no longer seen as being exclusively in the home, except by a small minority.

However, when one examines studies that investigate the attitudes and plans of women in more detail, it seems that the traditional viewpoint described earlier has not disappeared but, rather, has only been modified. The two major assumptions of this ideology are still accepted by a significant proportion of the population: the first being that a mother has primary responsibility for her child with the implication that separations are detrimental, and the second being that a woman receives primary fulfillment through her involvement with her family.

The motherhood mandate seems still to be in effect, with some revision. It might now be stated that children need full-time mothers to develop normally, but that this becomes less important as the children get older, especially once they enter school. Therefore, full-time motherhood, while perhaps desirable, is only essential in the child's first few years. Confirmation of this can be seen in the many studies that report negative attitudes toward working mothers of preschoolers and the minority of women who plan continuous careers.

The second tenet seems also to have been revised to some extent. It is now recognized that women have needs that are met through employment and that their careers are enriching and worthwhile. However, both men and women feel that women should place priority on their family roles, and the work role is still considered a secondary one. Few women are willing to place their careers ahead of family roles or to sacrifice marriage and motherhood for career success.

This is not to suggest that a sizable minority of men and women do not hold feminist views. Certainly there are men who are willing to restructure their own lives and goals to attempt to make equality between the sexes a reality. A growing number of couples now plan to remain childless (Hall and Hall, 1979), and many women do not place family roles above all else. However, for the majority of the American population of both sexes, the ideals of true sexual equality are accepted more in the abstract than in the reality of people's own lives. This can be clearly seen in the studies of dual-career families.

Dual-Career Families

So many millions of women and mothers are now in the labor force that increasing attention has been focused on two-worker families. Studied primarily through detailed case studies and in-depth interviews, investigations of these families have examined their backgrounds and histories, their perception and management of potential role conflicts, and the various costs and rewards attached to this pattern (Hall and Hall, 1979; Holmstrom, 1972; Rapoport and Rapoport, 1976). In this section, the focus will be primarily on how such couples perceive and cope with their dual roles, in an effort to explore the reality for those women who do attempt to combine both motherhood and employment.

Some investigators have differentiated between two-worker and dual-career families, the latter being a subset of the former. A career, according to Rapoport and Rapoport (1971), "designates those types of job sequences that require a high degree of commitment and that have a continuous developmental character . . . Thus, dual-career families, as compared with other two-worker families, tend to emphasize occupation as a primary source of personal fulfillment" (p. 21).

While those working in professional occupations are generally considered to have careers, Poloma and Garland (1971) argue that, in general, women may work in the professions but they do not have "careers"—with all the accompanying demands and degree of commitment—in the same sense as men do. However, most of the studies reported do deal with women who are professionals and college educated (as this present study does) and the authors, thus, generally refer to such women and their spouses as dual-career couples. Perhaps the distinction needs to be made between job commitment and priority of roles. One can be involved and committed to one's work while still not giving major priority to this role as opposed to others (Gannon and Hendrickson, 1973).

While an increasing number of such couples are choosing to remain childless (Hall and Hall, 1979), most combine their careers not only with marriage, but also with parenthood. As studies indicate, however, this combination is a difficult one. Despite the potential rewards and satisfactions, there is a great amount of strain and conflict involved in the attempt to combine roles (Herman and Gyllstrom, 1977; Holstrom, 1972; Rapoport and Rapoport, 1976). In a 1977 Quality of Employment Survey, for example, parents reported experiencing significantly more conflict than other couples. It was also reported that having preschool children was more stressful than having school-age children. More than one-third of all subjects with children indicated moderate or severe work-family conflicts (Pleck, Staines and Lang, 1980).

Further, much of the research shows that the strain, while present for all concerned (mother, father and children), is particularly severe for the mother. Johnson and Johnson (1977) interviewed 28 dual-career families with young children concerning career characteristics, marital power, child-rearing and family activities. They found that all the wives reported "major concerns over the conflict between their career and their children" (p. 393). Anxiety, guilt, fatigue and feelings of emotional depletion were common characteristics. These mothers were particularly concerned about the child's emotional needs; their physical needs were felt to be met satisfactorily. In contrast, husbands reported little role strain and when they did mention conflict, it was in a notably uninvolved manner. The authors felt that the source of strain for the women was related to childcare and not the marriage itself, and they concluded that "such processes were found irrespective of the amount of support the husbands were giving their wives in both emotional and practical areas, which was impressive in the majority of families" (p. 393).

Heckman, Bryson and Bryson (1977) studied 200 couples in which both partners were psychologists. They noted that husbands mentioned career/ home conflicts almost as much as their wives did. However, difficulties cited by husbands were often ones that had in fact been experienced by their wives. Because the problems affected their wives, they indirectly affected them as well. Conflicts mentioned by these couples included family versus job demands, role conflicts, bringing problems home and demands on time and energy.

In a cross-cultural study of businesswomen in India, Australia and Canada, Ross (1977) also reported that the strains these women experienced were directly related to meeting both motherhood and career demands.

A pilot study by the American Psychiatric Association compared 35 male psychiatrists with 35 female psychiatrists (Scher, Benedek, Candy, Carey, Mules and Sachs, 1976). Few differences were found except for family-career conflicts. Fifty percent of the women reported concerns about combining roles; the men did not.

Other studies, though, report no differences between the amount of family-career conflict for women as opposed to men. Herman and Gyllstrom (1977), for example, surveyed 500 employees of a major midwestern university including faculty, professional-academic, non-teaching and administrative personnel, and nonacademic clerical and technical personnel. The only differences between men and women were in the perceived conflict between work and home maintenance responsibilities. Women reported significantly greater conflict than men in this area. There were no differences between mothers and fathers on the amount of conflict reported between job and family responsibilities. (It was noted, however, that there were twice as many unmarried men in the sample as unmarried women.) Based on their findings, the authors suggested that inter-role conflict was not a function of sex, but rather of the number of social roles held.

It may be important, though, to consider what is meant by work-family conflicts. Pleck, Staines and Lang (1980) also report that employed husbands in their sample perceive nearly as much work-family conflict as do employed wives (although the margin is greater when there is a preschool child present). Differences emerge, however, when a closer look is taken at the reported source of the problem. Men indicate problems occurring more often as a result of excessive working hours—long hours and frequent overtime took time away from their families. Women, on the other hand, indicate that schedule incompatibilities as well as fatigue and irritability are their most commonly encountered difficulties, suggesting their greater responsibility for family tasks.

Thus, it appears that women who attempt to combine dual roles experience greater difficulties than their husbands. In part, this is the result of internalized norms and societal pressures regarding the appropriate role of women. The guilt and anxiety experienced may be a result of violating traditional norms. But such norms seem to be followed in reality as well, even for dual-career couples. Studies indicate that in the majority of cases, the woman retains responsibility for home activities, including childcare and housework, often leading them to describe themselves as having two full-time careers (Heckman, Bryson and Bryson, 1977; Rapoport and Rapoport, 1976; Zambrana, et al., 1979).

Johnson and Johnson (1977) report that the couples in their study were quite flexible and open to interchanging roles. They characterized eleven of the marriages as egalitarian, nine as husband-dominated and six as wife-dominated. In all cases but one, there was some degree of shared duty in the areas of childcare, scheduling and housework. However, all the wives retained the major responsibility in most areas of childrearing.

In a study of 53 couples in which the wife was a physician, attorney or college professor, Poloma and Garland (1971) found only one case which could be classified as truly egalitarian. In all other cases, the wife was expected (and expected herself) to see that the family ran smoothly. Despite career involvement, the home was considered the woman's major responsibility while the husband was responsible for being the main provider.

Data indicates that husbands of employed women do help with household tasks and childrearing more than do husbands of nonworking women (Hoffman and Nye, 1974); however, as already noted, the working wife still carries the greater share. Time budget studies in which the individual keeps a record of daily activities clearly support this conclusion. Meissner, Humphreys, Meis and Scheu (1975), for example, analyzed time budgets for 350 couples where both spouses worked. They report that the amount of hours spent in housework decreases if a woman works, although her total workload greatly increases. The decrease, however, is not compensated for by the husbands; the number of hours they contribute to household tasks remains the same regardless of the employment status of their wives. In effect, "the husband's contribution tends to be insensitive to increasing shared demands. . . . Men always work less than women in each of the strictly comparable conditions" (p. 429). In fact, the report noted that even the leisure-time experience of the men in the sample remained intact regardless of household requirements, with leisure-time activities (particularly television) actually increasing as their wives' workloads rose. Interestingly, many of the husbands in this study, as well as others (Poloma and Garland, 1971), spontaneously indicated that they felt men should help even less with housework in those cases where the wife chose to work, that is, was working for other than financial reasons. The authors conclude that "the condition of [the women's] dependency finds daily expression in the structure of the domestic working day . . . [it] leaves no exit for wives" (p. 431).

Thus, when faced with multiple role demands, it is the woman, more often than not, who has to deal with the conflicts (both time and emotional). Most of the women apparently deal with this strain by placing priority on family responsibilities. In study after study (Holmstrom, 1972; Pleck, 1977; Poloma, 1972; Rapoport and Rapoport, 1976) the most common coping mechanism used by wives was to assign priority to domestic roles. This was true not only when there were conflicts between the children and the woman's career, but also when the conflicts involved the husband's career. "The tendency is still for women to subordinate their own career aspirations to those of their husbands and to defer their own involvements in the world of work until they have attended to the conventional requirements of childbearing. . . . [Any other] arrangement is unusual, even today" (Rapoport and Rapoport, 1976, p. 20). Poloma (1972) remarks that the women in her study were aware "of the fact that their professional involvement had less priority than their husbands' and was more subject to fluctuations in family demands. This was viewed as being essential to making a dual-profession family work. . . . Some women observed that, given our present society, it is impossible to combine a career in the real sense of the term (uninterrupted, full-time work with a high degree of commitment) with the demands of a family" (p. 193-94).

Pleck (1977) in an essay exploring the work-family role system, hypothesizes that there are limits to how much changes in one role will affect the other roles to which it is linked. He suggests the existence of two buffers: the first being a sex-segregated market, the second, asymmetrically permeable boundaries between work and family roles for both sexes. It is the latter mechanism which is of relevance to this review. Pleck asserts that although work and family roles are interrelated, they function differently for men and women. For women, family roles are allowed, if not expected, to affect work roles. Demands of the former intrude on performance of the latter since the family takes priority for most women. The reverse is true for most men. In their case, it is work roles which are allowed and expected to interfere with the performance of family roles and it is the family which is expected to accommodate if the workload increases.

This situation has meant, for many women, an interruption of their careers at those times when family demands increase. The transition into parenthood, in particular, has been the time when many women, even those in dual-career families, drop out of the labor force (Hall and Hall, 1979). In Poloma's (1972) study of 45 such families, for example, 28 of the wives—all high status professionals—did not work at all before their children were in school; another ten worked only part-time. Other investigators (Heckman, et al., 1977; Lewin and Damrell, 1978; Rossi, 1972) report similar statistics.

Dropping out of the labor force, even for relatively short periods of time, and/or cutting back on career involvement to meet growing family demands, are not without implications. The consequences, particularly for the woman's career, can be quite serious. The time when most women interrupt their careers (late twenties and early thirties) is precisely the time when most men are establishing themselves in theirs. For many types of work, it is also the time of greatest productivity. Rossi (1972) notes that, at least in the sciences, the peak of creative work is reached during these years. The loss of knowledge, especially in those fields where technological changes are rapidly occurring, is certainly of concern, as is the difficulty of advancement. As Rapoport and Rapoport (1971) note, "it is difficult for women to rise into positions of senior responsibility once they have dropped out . . . however unprejudiced the work environment may be and however competent the women may be" (p. 22).

The effects on income also have become apparent. Hudis (1976) argues that differences in earnings for men and women are attributable, in part, to women's competing roles. Interrupted labor force participation and familial constraints result in married women receiving smaller economic benefits from schooling and occupational status.

This situation is not only costly for the women themselves but also for society, as many well-educated women drop out of the labor market just after they have acquired years of training and experience and are becoming most valuable. In addition, it perpetuates the status quo whereby women rarely reach upper-level, policy-making positions.

Despite these negative implications, there is little evidence that this system is not favored by the majority of women. Poloma and Garland (1971), for instance, report that the women in their sample had made a conscious decision to give priority to their husband's careers and family responsibilities, and were content with the situation. "In exchange for the limitations placed on their careers, these wives had financial security provided by their husbands as breadwinners, while the women themselves enjoyed the option of working or not working" (p. 536). They perceived themselves, in effect, as having the best of both worlds.

Summary

While there is increasingly widespread suport for women pursuing careers, societal norms still dictate that this occur only if and/or after a woman has fulfilled her traditional responsibilities. This review of dual-career families indicates that this is a norm that most women adhere to. In studies of relatively high-status, professional women, it becomes clear that combining dual roles is no easy task. Practical difficulties, normative sanctions and internalized attitudes and expectations result in conflict and strains that are particularly severe for the woman. Attempts to resolve such potential conflict generally involve giving traditional family roles priority. While this has negative implications for the woman, her career and society, it appears that most women, as well as their husbands, prefer this solution.

Motivational Factors

Given the ambivalent norms about women's roles and the many problems involved in dual-career families, one might wonder why women work at all, especially if they have young children. Sociocultural changes in past decades—expanded economy, lower birth rates, higher educational levels, advanced technology—certainly have resulted in a climate which is more conducive to working women in general. Career patterns, not surprisingly, have been statistically related to many demographic features—education, number of children, ages of children, husband's income, race, etc. (Hoffman, 1974). However, individual motivations—why a particular woman in a given circumstance decides to work or not to work at a particular time—are much less well-understood, despite the fact that such information is critical to the comprehension of the phenomenon itself, and of its effects on the woman, her husband and children, and on society (Hoffman, 1974).

Unfortunately, there has been little direct investigation of individual motivations for employment. Data regarding demographic, psychological and social differences between women who work and those who don't are more available (and will be reviewed in the next section) but necessitate a causal leap to infer underlying motives. The following section will review what data is available as well as suggest potential motivating factors that may be involved in the decision either to work or not to work.

Motivations for Employment

While women work for a variety of reasons, financial factors are probably the most commonly cited; this may be especially true of women with young children. Rosenfeld and Perella (1965), for example, found that in a national sample of working women, 41 percent of the women surveyed said that "financial necessity" was the most important reason for their entering the labor force. An additional 7 percent cited husband's loss of job and 17 percent said the major reason was to "earn extra money." Thus, the dominant motive reported for 65 percent of the sample was economically related. For women with children under six, the number was even higher—

72 percent cited financial motivations. Personal satisfaction was the major reason given for 19 percent of the women but only 12 percent of those with young children.

Hoffman (1974) estimates that when asked why they work, anywhere between 55 percent and 90 percent of the women will respond in terms of money. She also notes, however, that financial necessity or even added income has been one of the most socially acceptable reasons available for working women; thus, many might respond in this manner to avoid social sanction. Certainly, studies of attitudes toward working mothers that have been reviewed previously support this hypothesis. There is little disagreement today that it is acceptable for mothers, even those of young children, to work because of financial need.

Of course, perception of financial need varies with the situation and the individual. Working mothers are indeed often the sole or main support of the family—particularly in cases of divorce. Yet economic motivations involve more than critical financial need. Clearly, perceived financial need, income satisfaction and desire for a particular standard of living all are important factors. This may be particularly true for women with young children. With the dramatic rise in inflation in recent years, the incomes of both spouses have become particularly important. A young couple may get accustomed to a certain standard of living or have accumulated debts during this period. When their first child is born, they may not feel they can afford to lose one income, although statistically they may be well above the national median income. Such a woman works because of financial reasons which are quite different from those of the divorced mother whose ex-husband does not provide child support.

Hall and Hall (1979) report that (1) a 1964 study found that two-thirds of working mothers were employed out of economic need, while only one-sixth were working for personal satisfaction, (2) in 1974, a National Opinion Research Center Survey reported that only 15 percent to 25 percent of mothers gave high income as their most preferred job characteristic, with 60 percent listing "meaningful work," and (3) in a more recent survey, 80 percent of the 18 to 34 year old women said they would continue to work even if money were not a problem. Hence, they conclude, despite the fact that these studies are not truly comparable, motivations of women (for employment) are changing.

However, a recent national poll (Carmichael, 1980) found that income is still the primary reason given by women for employment. Forty-three percent said they were working to supplement the family income, 27 percent responded that they were working to support themselves and 19 percent to support the family. Only 14 percent said they were primarily working "for something interesting to do." While the figures are not broken down by age of children, it would seem reasonable to assume, given the results of prior studies (Hoffman, 1974), that financial motivations are an even greater factor for women with children under six.

Despite the fact that income is still a strong motivating factor, it certainly is not the only one. Women at all income levels are entering the labor force; in fact, the labor force rate has risen more for women in the upper than in the lower income brackets. For example, between 1960 and 1977, the number of employed women with children under six rose 66 percent for those women whose husbands' incomes were in the lowest quartile nationally. The relative change for women whose husbands' earned in the upper quartile was 134 percent (Ryscavage, 1979). Of course, the base rate for this group was lower and they still do not participate in the labor force as much as do women who are at the lower income levels. Still, it is clear that while money, or rather the lack of it, is an important precipitating factor, other considerations enter in as well.

Perhaps one of the difficulties in this area of research is a methodological one. Hoffman (1974) points out that while data is often based on the responses to a single question, motivations for employment are complex and multifaceted. Even in Rosenfeld and Perrella's study (1965), only 25 percent of the mothers of young children indicated they would stop working if money were not a factor.

In another study (Parnes, Shea, Spitz and Zeller, 1970), a deliberate effort was made to delve beyond monetary motives by asking subjects if they would continue to work if they had enough money. Among married white women, 50 percent of mothers with preschool children and 56 percent of mothers with older children said they would. Reasons given were boredom, companionship and personal satisfaction. Those who would not continue to work cited the desire to spend more time with their families.

In a recent study, Salo (1977) asked employed women with young children to indicate their reasons for working. Sixty-one percent cited financial reasons while only 27 percent gave more personal reasons (12 percent indicated personal fulfillment, 6 percent liked contact with others and 9 percent wanted to pursue outside interests) as their major motivation. However, personal fulfillment was given as the second reason for 43 percent of the subjects.

Thus it would seem that, while financial motivations are extremely important, other factors are involved for a significant proportion of working women, even those with young children. While raising a child can be a very creative, rewarding experience, it may also be very frustrating. Childrearing involves many repetitive, often boring, tasks and housework significantly adds to the tedium In addition, the mother often must defer her own satisfactions in favor of the child's needs and she may long for a change of scenery and adult company. Some research, for example, has indicated that childrearing is associated with greater stress and mental illness (Seiden, 1976). The loss of freedom inherent in raising a young child may therefore be a motivation for working. A 1966 study of college educated women showed that 12 percent of women with children under six gave "to escape household routine" as their major reason for working (Hoffman, 1974).

Rossman and Campbell (1965) studied factors which they hypothesized would precipitate employment if other conditions were facilitative (e.g., high education and available job opportunities). They concluded that factors such as lower marital satisfaction, lower income and lower life satisfaction would operate in the decision to work outside the home. They seem to suggest that employment may therefore be motivated by a woman's dissatisfaction with her present situation.

The potential gratifications of work—self-fulfillment, independence, achievement, putting one's education into effect—are also major motivating forces. In fact, it is nonfinancial reasons such as these that are generally related to a woman's work commitment. While commitment has been defined in various ways, including future work plans (Sobol, 1974), desire for continued or future employment (Haller and Rosenmayer, 1971) and the relative distribution of interest, time and energy devoted to work in relation to other life sectors (Safilios-Rothschild, 1970), it is generally recognized that work commitment is an important variable in considering which women engage in continuous work involvement and the effects of employment on all concerned.

Sobol (1974) notes that women who give nonfinancial reasons for work have a greater likelihood of maintaining continued attachment to the labor force than women who give a combination of monetary and other motivations. The most committed women were working to fill a need for accomplishment, to meet people or to occupy time. Eyde (1968) and Baruch (1967) also found that women with high needs for achievement indicate the strongest motivation to work.

Fuchs (1971), in a study of West German women, indicated that a greater percentage of women with high work commitment reported personal motives for employment. He further noted that these women also like housekeeping and are satisfied with their life planning. Perhaps it is the women who are committed to long-term job involvement who work primarily for personal reasons such as a desire for achievement, while other women may work because of negative aspects of their present lives—low income, dissatisfaction with housework or boredom.

Motivations for Not Working

The decision not to work would also seem to be the result of complex, multifaceted factors. Many women feel it is important for them to stay home for the sake of their child. This is especially true for mothers of infants and preschoolers. Simmons (1970), for example, held intensive interviews with a number of professionally trained women regarding their attitudes toward working and found that the main reason some of the mothers did not want to work was concern for their child. These mothers expressed strong fears about the child's sense of security, believed that a babysitter could not substitute for a mother and worried about the mother-child bond. They felt that, if they worked, they could not give their children the amount of love and attention they required.

Hock (1978) questioned mothers of three-month-old infants regarding their perceptions of their baby's needs. She found that working mothers were less likely to perceive infant distress at separation, felt less anxiety about leaving their infants and were less apprehensive about substitute care. Those nonworking mothers who were highly career-oriented were the most likely to perceive infant distress at separation caused by the mother's leaving. Noting that specific separation anxiety is usually not seen until five or six months, she concludes that the nonworking mothers' perceptions were consistent with their beliefs about the need for an exclusive mother-child relationship and that the women seemed to refrain from working out of a sense of duty. Consistent with this is a study by Birnbaum (1975) in which she notes that full-time homemakers, as compared to professional women, more often emphasized the sacrifice that motherhood entailed and to a greater extent stressed duty and responsibility.

Motherhood is also generally an extremely fulfilling experience and many women feel that they can best enjoy this experience by remaining home full-time with their youngsters. In Simmons's (1970) study, many of the women mentioned "selfish" reasons for not working. They wanted to be with their child as much as possible in order "not to miss anything" and enjoyed "seeing themselves reflected." Further, they felt a need for the close bond that develops between mother and child and enjoyed the attachment. Simmons suggests that those mothers may have had a greater need to feel needed and loved by their children and were less confident of this attachment being sustained if they were not at home full-time.

Salo (1977) asked full-time mothers to give their reasons for not returning to their careers after the birth of their child. Eighty-one percent said their primary reason was they "wanted to stay home with the child." The second ranked item was that "the child was too young"; 52 percent gave this as their second reason, with 8 percent ranking it first. Thus, for these mothers, it would seem that their own need to be with the child was the primary consideration.

In addition, many women enjoy the daily home experience. They may find it offers more autonomy than a job, giving them a chance to be on their own and to engage in activities they previously had no time for. The flexibility and freedom to pursue one's own interests can be quite appealing, especially for those women who expect to return to the labor force sometime in the future.

For women with preschool children, it may be extremely difficult to work full-time even if one prefers to. The lack of quality day-care, for instance, and its often prohibitive cost, may make it almost impossible for a conscientious mother to work outside the home. Doing so might even result in a loss of income, after day-care and housekeeping costs are taken into account.

It is also possible that some women may remain at home because of their own concerns and fears about participating in the work world. Horner (1972), for example, postulates a "fear of success" among able college women. She suggests that some women may avoid success because they anticipate accompanying negative consequences such as social rejection or loss of femininity. This might be avoided by remaining in the roles considered most suitable for women.

Conversely, some women may choose not to return to work after they have a child because of low self-esteem. O'Leary (1974) and Disabatino (1976) suggest that women who have little confidence in their abilities may avoid career involvement. Dissatisfaction with previous work involvement or lack of success in their chosen field may also make the homemaker role seem considerably more attractive at any particular point in time.

Husband's Attitude

While there is little direct evidence bearing on the relationship between a woman's motivation for employment and her husband's attitude, it has been widely suggested that spouse approval is critical if a woman is to continue her career (Epstein, 1970; Hawley, 1978; Holmstrom, 1972; Rapoport and Rapoport, 1976). Bailyn (1964) called men's attitudes the most important source of support or hostility for the professional woman.

Weil (1961) in her study of factors influencing the actual or planned participation of women in the labor force, concluded that the determining factors were the career orientation of the wife and the favorable attitude of the husband. Wise and Carter (1965) reported that the factor most influencing a woman's attitude toward employment was her perception of her husband's attitude. Yockey (1975) suggests that women who are employed will perceive their husbands as holding positive expectations for female autonomy. This, in turn, reinforces their own tendencies.

Arnott (1972), in a somewhat complex investigation, studied attitude congruency between husband and wife and the effect of the wife's attitude toward autonomy on conflict resolution. They report that shared role preference was associated with a high degree of role stability. Few of the women indicated that they would be willing to oppose their husbands' wishes. Those women holding "liberal" attitudes reported being more willing to do so than the "conservatives"; still, only one-third said they would face this opposition if necessary. In addition, there was a strong tendency to perceive the husband's attitude in line with one's own. This occurred either through the misperception of the husband's attitude or the expectation that his attitude was changing. The author concludes that while "the influence of the husband's attitude was unquestionable, it did not generally seem to have the impact that self-concept has on role involvement. . . . It should be noted, however, that husband's influence rose when preferences conflicted. . . . The reasons given for inability to enter a desired role, and the women's stated reluctance to oppose their husbands . . . underscores the difficulty women have in facing overt opposition" (p. 683).

Thus it would seem that the attitudes of her husband influence a woman's participation in the labor force and the intensity of her commitment. This, of course, can work both ways. A woman may remain at home, in part, because of her husband's wishes. On the other hand, a woman may begin or continue working because of her husband's support. In fact, it is certainly possible that the husband may be more interested in having his wife involved in work than the woman is herself.

Summary

Clearly there are a multitude of factors involved in a woman's decision to work or remain home. While income is widely cited as the primary reason for the employment of women, it is clear that other factors come into play in this decision. Perhaps one might conceptualize this choice as being based on a combination of perceived benefits and costs.

If there is a clear financial need, for example, the woman will generally work regardless of whether or not she would ideally like to. If there is some financial benefit (i.e., the added income would maintain a high standard of living), other perceived advantages of employment (e.g., chance for achievement, satisfaction, career advancement) will lead to labor force participation; without them, the financial considerations would not be enough. If income is clearly not a realistic factor, however (i.e., husband is in the high income bracket), then the more personal benefits of employment need to be extremely salient for a woman to work.

The barriers to working are perhaps most apparent for the woman when she has a young child. It is at this time that social norms are especially negative. Here too, however, a woman's own (and her husband's) attitude regarding the needs of the child and her desire to remain at home will determine how great this disadvantage is. For those who strongly believe that a child needs a full-time mother, the benefits of working would have to be extremely high for them to consider employment, while for those who do not hold this belief, the attractions of work would not need to be as salient.

Comparison of Working and Nonworking Women

As employment by women has become increasingly common and publicly visible, a number of investigators have focused on the question of what distinguishes women who work outside the home from those who do not. Demographic, experiential, personality and attitudinal variables have all been examined in an effort to uncover underlying differences in these populations. The emphases of such studies vary; some attempt to ascertain factors that might influence particular women to choose a career (or joint family-career) versus homemaking pattern, while others emphasize the ramifications of this choice—how each pattern affects the woman herself and her family.

For purposes of this review, our primary interest is in the first group of studies, those that explore familial, personality and attitudinal differences between working and nonworking women in an effort to further elucidate motivational factors. In other words, are there group differences that might explain why some women work while others do not?

Unfortunately, research in this area has not been abundant, perhaps because, until recently, a working pattern was rare and attention was more directly focused on norms regarding this issue and the potential effects of the "deviant" pattern.

Background Characteristics

A variety of demographic variables have been found to reliably differentiate working from nonworking women. Employed women are more likely to have fewer children, older children, more education and lower family incomes (Harmon, 1970; Hoffman and Nye, 1974; U.S. Dept. of Commerce, 1979). The temporal ordering of life events also varies; for example, career women work longer before marrying, may delay having children and generally have fewer children (Harmon, 1970; Helson, 1972).

Family background has been investigated by a number of researchers. Rapoport and Rapoport (1971), for example, in a pioneer study of dual-career families in England, extensively interviewed and observed couples in which both partners had demanding careers. They found that there were a number of similarities in the family backgrounds of the women. As a group, they tended to come from a higher social class than their husbands and to have had smaller families. They were much more likely than other women to have had mothers who worked and who enjoyed working, or if their mothers were homemakers, they were more likely to have been dissatisfied and frustrated with their roles than the mothers of conventional women. Further, the Rapoports noted that many of these women were the oldest or only child in the family and experienced significant elements of tension within the family, including the tendency for early separations. These factors contributed to what the authors term the "only-lonely child pattern." However, there was generally also a significant adult in the picture with whom a warm, close relationship developed.

Kriger (1972), in a study comparing college-educated homemakers, women in traditional, female-dominated occupations, and those in pioneer, male-dominated fields, hypothesized that family dynamics affect a woman's basic career development. Postulating that a woman's primary career decision involves whether or not to work at all (presumably after the first child) and is a function of the parents' mode of childrearing, she measured women's perceptions of their parents' attitudes. Homemakers were found to perceive their parents as controlling, restrictive and overprotective, while the working women saw their parents as permissive and accepting. There were no differences between the perceptions of women working in traditional versus nontraditional fields.

Birnbaum (1975) in an extensive investigation of the background, personality style and self-esteem of middle-aged homemakers, married professionals and single professionals, found that the three groups tended to have distinct family backgrounds. The homemaker generally came from a successful, traditional middle-class family, in which her father was the provider and her mother a housewife. Both parents were relatively well-educated, but neither was particularly intellectual. The father is remembered as somewhat distant, the mother as nonassertive. Both parents expected their daughter to marry an achieving spouse and valued the traditional feminine traits as opposed to intellectual achievement. In contrast, the married professional was raised in a relatively nontraditional middle- or upper-class family. Both parents were generally highly educated. The father often had a graduate or professional degree and is remembered as being intellectual and close to his daughter. The mother often worked outside the home and is seen as having been competitive and dominant but also very dependent on and very close to her family. Both parents valued competence and academic achievement in their daughter. The single professional, on the other hand, typically came from a lower-middle- or lower-class background. Her parents had generally not gone beyond high school and were traditionally oriented. While both parents are remembered as particularly attractive, they were neither intellectual nor dependent and their daughter was not very close to either one. Appearance was clearly emphasized over academic achievement.

Other studies also indicate that working women, particularly professional women, share certain family background characteristics. The women in Ginzberg's (1971) study generally described their fathers as supportive and achievement oriented, Hennig (1973) observed that the women executives she researched were likely to be the oldest child in their families and Hoffman (1974) notes the relationship between maternal employment and the daughter's own career plans. Bielby (1978), however, reports that background variables, particularly mothers' employment, account for only a small percentage of the variance between groups.

Personality Characteristics

Personality variables thought to distinguish between working and non-working women have been the subject of several investigations. Hoffman (1974), for example, reviewed studies examining the hypothesis that working women have greater needs for power and dominance and concluded that empirical evidence did not support this idea. Two variables that do seem to differentiate working women from homemakers are achievement needs and self-esteem, although evidence is still far from conclusive.

Eyde (1968) and Sobol (1974) both suggest that work commitment is related to a need for achievement; however, this is not characteristic of women who do not indicate a high motivation for employment but do expect to work in the future (presumably due to financial considerations). Kriger (1972), however, using the achievement scale of the Edwards Personal Preference Schedule, found that homemakers were indeed less achievement oriented than the working women in her study. Studies by Steinmann (1974) and Ohlbaum (1971) support this orientation toward achievement in working women.

Evidence contradictory to these findings was reported by Birnbaum (1971) who utilized a projective measure of achievement. Shelton (1967) measured achievement motivation of housewives and professional women through both the TAT and the Test of Insight. He found significant differences in the predicted direction only on the latter.

It is possible that this contradictory evidence is a result of using different measures of achievement. Hoffman (1974) suggests that while professional women may be characterized by high achievement needs, these needs are not revealed in projective measures which may be more sensitive to unmet psychological needs. In addition, it is possible that homemakers do have high achievement needs but attempt to meet them vicariously through their husbands.

The second area in which personality differences have emerged is that of self-esteem and personal identity. Birnbaum (1975), for example, reports clear differences in this regard with the college-educated women she studied. She observes that the typical homemaker is conventional and dependent, avoids aggression and assertiveness and is directed toward love, nurturance and self-sacrifice. Of the three groups she studied, the homemakers had the lowest self-esteem and the lowest sense of personal competence, even in regard to childcare and social skills, the areas in which their primary energies were focused. They felt less attractive, were most concerned about self-identity issues and indicated frequent feelings of loneliness. They reported missing a sense of challenge and creative involvement in their lives. The married professional, on the other hand, was unconventional, competitive and not at all self-sacrificing. While she rated herself as equally dependent as the homemaker, she was much more satisfied with herself and her life circumstances. Her self-esteem was high and she felt competent and worthwhile in all spheres of her life.

O'Connell (1976) studied identity formation in three groups of college-educated women: traditional (full-time homemakers); neotraditional (those who returned to paid employment when their children were older); and nontraditonal (women who simultaneously combined their careers with childrearing). She found that the three groups of women perceived their identities in different ways. Nontraditional women reported a strong sense of personal identity throughout their adult lives, an identity which continued to grow stronger. A personal identity was defined as "an awareness of, and emphasis upon, one's talents, endowments, capabilities and needs; its focus is on one's unique qualities from which one's self-esteem and feelings of worth are derived" (p. 676). In contrast, both traditional and neotraditional women felt their personal identities were not very strong at adolescence and shifted to a more reflected identity after marriage and childbirth. A reflected sense of identity "emphasizes the significant others in one's life; its focus is external . . . it is sense of identity by association" (p. 676). Thus, home-makers seemed to experience a moratorium on personal identity at least until their children were older; nontraditional women do not.

Ohlbaum (1971) compared working professionals with homemakers on measures of self-actualization, self-concepts and values. She reports that the professional women had more positive self-concepts with a greater degree of personal autonomy and self-esteem and a higher level of self-actualization. The homemakers expressed their dissatisfaction with themselves and their frustration over their lack of growth and development.

Other studies (Broverman, et. al., 1972; Yockey, 1975) also report higher self-esteem and feelings of competence in working women as compared to homemakers.

Stake (1979), however, suggests that self-esteem mediates the relationship between attitudes and career commitment. While high self-esteem was associated with higher career motivation, the main finding of her study was that those with high self-esteem were able to resolve the home-career conflict in a manner consistent with their preferences. Those who indicated the strongest career motivation, for instance, had a lifestyle that was consistent with this, while those with more traditional attitudes indicated a more moderate level of career interest. For those women with low self-esteem, there was little relationship between career motivation and their lifestyle. Stake concludes that "women who have little confidence in their abilities will have more difficulty coming to grips with the conflicts of home and career" (p. 40).

Other studies (Lahat-Mandelbaum, 1976; Salo, 1977) report finding little or no personality differences between working and nonworking women. Thus, it would seem that, as Hoffman (1974) concludes, "It is premature to say whether or not personality traits differentiate working from nonworking women ..." (p. 52).

Unfortunately, methodological problems make it difficult to compare the results of various studies. Besides the fact that different instruments are used to measure variables, the populations examined are not comparable. While most of the reported studies are investigating college-educated women, ages of the women, family stage, presence of children and type of occupations studied vary from study to study. Perhaps even more critical is that the population within a particular study is often too heterogeneous for meaningful comprehension of data. There may be little control for variables already mentioned such as age, occupation and number of children. In addition, whether the woman is working full-or part-time, has worked continuously throughout her life or has interrupted her career for various periods, and is motivated to work by personal or financial reasons is often not taken into consideration. Thus, it is possible that studies which report no differences between working and nonworking women may have taken too broad a view of working women. As Hoffman suggests,

> It is not meaningful to try to describe the personality characteristics that distinguish working mothers. The pattern is too widespread and the group too heterogeneous. However, comparisons between working and nonworking mothers in the same situation, with comparable education and family incomes, at the same stage in the family cycle, with the same number of children, and with equal opportunities for employment, should reveal personality differences. [p. 49]

Attitudinal Variables

Sex-role attitudes has been a variable of interest and a number of studies have differentiated working from nonworking women in this area, concluding that working women hold more liberal views of sex roles (Birnbaum, 1971; Ohlbaum, 1971; Parnes, et al., 1970).

Weil (1961), in a relatively early study of working and nonworking suburban mothers, reported that there was a relationship between employment and having a companionship-type marriage. In addition, there was a relationship between the level of employment, plans for employment and the companionship role. There was a steady and marked decline of women classified in this role as work status went from working full-time to working part-time to planning to work in the future to not planning to work at all. Furthermore, the working women had husbands who were more likely to accept an obligation for childcare and household chores.

Angrist (1966), on the other hand, reports no differences on a measure of sex-role ideology between college-educated women who were working and those who were not. She concludes that "neither the specific constellation of roles a woman carries out, nor the potential enactment of these roles, are necessarily indicative of the attitudes these women hold" (p. 455). Hopkins (1977) and Nagely (1971) also found few attitudinal differences between groups.

Perhaps one reason for these contradictory findings lies in attempting to associate sex-role attitudes with behavior. These variables are not necessarily synonymous. Bielby (1978), for example, found that sex-role ideology was positively related to career commitment but not to full-time employment. Another difficulty may also result from investigating groups that are too heterogeneous. Safilios-Rothschild (1970) hypothesizes, for example, that the relationship between employment status and family dynamics is mediated by the degree of work commitment exhibited by the wife. She found that employed women with high commitment had significantly more favorable attitudes toward working women while there were no differences between the attitudes held by working women with low commitment (who were working primarily for monetary reasons) and homemakers. While her study examined the attitudes and behaviors of Greek women, it is presumable that a similar relationship between work commitment or motivation for employment and attitudinal variables exists for American women as well.

Husbands' Characteristics

Although it has been suggested that spouse approval is critical if a woman is to continue her career, there have been few studies that have explored characteristics of husbands of working or nonworking women.

Rapoport and Rapoport (1976) did note that the only experiential factor that apparently differentiated the husbands in the dual-career families was their particularly close relationships to their mothers. "Though pronounced [it] was not so emphatic as to give it a pathogenic character . . . Rather, a pattern of warmth and sympathy seems to have been established that may have laid the foundations for a subsequent responsiveness to the aspirations of their wives" (p. 44).

In addition, it was personally important to these men, for various reasons, that their wives develop their careers. They each had a strong emotional investment in this and wanted their wives to continue working.

The women were thus able to perceive their work as for "the overall benefit of the family and not simply as a selfish personal wish" (p. 296).

The men in this particular study were also relatively family-oriented. Women married to men whose careers are all-important and to whom family matters are clearly secondary are not likely to work, especially if they have young children (Scher, et al., 1976). Bailyn (1970) argues that "an educated, married woman's resolution of the 'career-family' dilemma cannot be adequately evaluated without knowledge of her husband's resolution—of the way he fits his work and his family into his life" (p. 97). In a study of 200 British families, she found little relation between husbands' and wives' career versus family orientations. Women who hoped to integrate both roles were no more likely to be married to men who placed primacy on their families than to men with career orientations. However, when these women married career-oriented men, their marriages tended not to be very happy. On the other hand, a successful marriage was likely to result when a woman who expected to coordinate dual roles for herself was married to a man for whom primary emphasis was on the family, although his work was still considered to be both important and satisfying. Safilios-Rothschild's work (1976) supports this assumption.

The professional married women in Birnbaum's (1975) study described their husbands as particularly supportive. In fact, she notes that these husbands are portrayed not only as responsive and sensitive but also as brilliant, superior men deserving of unqualified, glowing admiration. The author suggests that, whether reality-based or not, it was essential for these women to perceive their husbands as superior in order to avoid any competitiveness. "Thus while the married professional is certainly psychologically freer than most women to seek personal distinction, it seems that she is free to do her very best only because she is convinced that her husband can do still better" (p. 413).

In one of the only empirical investigations of personality factors of husbands, Burke and Weir (1976) examined interpersonal need structures of both husbands and wives in traditional families and dual-career families. Utilizing the Fundamental Interpersonal Relations Orientation Inventory, it was found that both partners in the dual-career families had significantly lower needs for social interchange in the areas of affection, inclusion and control and were more self-reliant, self-sufficient individuals. The working wives were more self-assertive than the housewives but husbands of working wives were less assertive and less concerned with power and authority than the husbands of housewives. The latter were the most concerned with authority and dominance and least concerned with developing affiliations and feelings of togetherness and involvement. The authors conclude that "members of dual-career families may be better suited to a collegial type of marriage relationship which would allow for the development of separate identities and for a sharing of power between the partners, in addition to meeting their lower relational needs" (p. 458).

Summary

While a number of studies have reported substantial differences between working mothers and homemakers in background characteristics, attitudes toward women's roles and personality variables such as self-esteem and achievement orientations, the data is often inconsistent and certainly inconclusive.

A variety of methodological problems that may lie behind these inconsistencies have already been discussed. Primarily these involve attempts to classify women as working or not working when, in fact, this dichotomy is too broad to be very meaningful. It has been suggested that it might be more fruitful to explore characteristics of a small, more homogeneous population.

Another difficulty inherent in studies of this sort lies in the attempt to attribute causality to any significant differences found between groups. It is generally not possible to ascertain whether these women self-selected themselves into the various groups based on previously existing differences in personality and attitudes or whether these differences are the result of being employed. For example, perhaps when women enter the labor force, their attitudes about the proper role of women change as a direct result of their own experience. This is quite different from assuming that a more modern ideology induces women to seek employment. Likewise, high self-esteem may lead to a woman seeking outside sources of fulfillment or it may be the result of successfully engaging in paid employment. Longitudinal studies would seem necessary to sort out these opposing hypotheses. At the least, to increase our understanding of motivational factors, we need to learn more about how working women (and their husbands) differ from non-working women (and their husbands) at the point of making their decision regarding employment (Hoffman, 1974).

Comparison of Career-Oriented and Homemaking-Oriented College Women

Related to research comparing working women and homemakers is data exploring determinants of women's orientations toward a career or homemaking pattern. With the emphasis primarily on college women, investigators have focused on many of the same factors discussed above—background, personality and attitudinal variables—and have tended to affirm the relation of a number of these to career orientation or commitment.

While each study uses somewhat different operational definitions, a career orientation may be viewed broadly as an active interest in preparing for a career and an intention to work in the future, although it does not necessarily imply an expectation of a continuous work involvement. A homemaking orientation, on the other hand, is considered to involve only minimal preparation for a career with little or no plans for employment beyond the childbearing stages.

Despite the fact that it is difficult to predict a woman's future employment from her orientations in college (Harmon, 1970), more research has been focused on this group than on actual working women or on homemakers. Presumably this is because college students have always been more easily accessible to researchers. In addition, it was hoped that this area of research would illuminate the process of career development in women and would contribute to an understanding of motivational factors that lead to later employment. However, research dealing with hypothesized future orientations has been separated in this review from studies based on actual behavior because it is believed that the two sets of data, while related, are not completely comparable.

Backgound Characteristics

The importance of the parents has often been hypothesized to relate to a woman's career or home orientation, with maternal employment being a particular focus of interest. It has been suggested that role expectations may be transmitted from mother to daughter by a process of identification. If the mother's role behaviors include employment, then it is likely that her daughter will perceive a career as an appropriate role for women. Studies have indeed shown that maternal employment is correlated with daughter's future work plans (Almquist and Angrist, 1970; Hoffman, 1974; Stein, 1973).

In addition, maternal employment implies somewhat less restricted sex-role definitions and should therefore influence the child's perceptions of sex-role differentiation. Research has supported this hypothesis too, showing that college students whose mothers are employed perceive less differentiation and stereotyping of masculine and feminine characteristics and behaviors (Vogel, et al., 1970) and are less likely to devalue female competence (Baruch, 1972).

However, further investigation has revealed that there is not a simple, clear correlation between maternal employment and daughter's career commitment. Rather, this relationship is mediated by the mother's satisfaction with her status, whether employed or not, and her daughter's perceptions of this. Baruch (1972), for example, studied college women at a prestigious eastern college and found that maternal employment per se did not affect attitudes toward a dual role pattern. What did influence the daughters' attitudes were their mothers' feelings about combining career and family roles. Further, the mother's ability to successfully integrate the various roles, if she did work, was an important variable. Another study (Baruch, 1973) supported this conclusion; while maternal employment was not positively related to self-esteem or perception of the subjects' own competence, the mother's preference for a career, in addition to family responsibilities, was.

Altman and Grossman (1977) further refined this relationship. In their examination of senior women enrolled in a large urban university, they found that daughters of working, career-oriented women did show a greater career orientation than daughters of home-oriented housewives. Exploring further, they established that daughters of homemakers were likely to want to emulate this orientation if they believed their mothers were satisfied with their family role, while daughters who perceived their mothers as dissatisfied with homemaking were more likely to be career-oriented, attributing this dissatisfaction to the mother's singular life-focus. However, the relationship between perception of maternal satisfaction and life goals was more complicated for daughters of employed women. Those who perceived their working mothers as dissatisfied were still career-oriented. The authors felt that the dissatisfied working mothers, in this case, were not unhappy with the combination of dual roles as much as they were frustrated with their jobs. The daughters then were even more likely to want to achieve a greater career-potential to avoid their mothers' dissatisfaction.

Thus the mother's own orientation and satisfaction with her life seem to be more important than her employment status. If the mother is seen as satisfied, her daughter is likely to identify with her and want to follow in her footsteps. If the mother is perceived as dissatisfied, however, her daughter's plans will be more dependent on her interpretation of the reasons behind this dissatisfaction.

Other background variables have been studied as well. For example, researchers have reported that women who are highly career-oriented and plan on nontraditional, continuous careers are more often firstborn children (Hennig, 1973; Stewart and Winter, 1974; Tangri, 1972) and have had fathers who encouraged independence and with whom these girls were highly identified, although not necessarily close. (Ginzberg, 1971; Oliver, 1975; Standley and Soule, 1974).

Personality Characteristics

As with investigations of actual working women and homemakers, personality variables that have been hypothesized to differentiate career-oriented women from home-oriented women have been explored. It is anticipated that these differences would be indicative of motivational factors involved in the development of career or family interests.

An early study by Hoyt and Kennedy (1958) found that career- and home-oriented college women showed different sets of interests on the Strong Vocational Interest Blank. It was hypothesized that these patterns reflected differences on a "professional orientation" dimension. The authors also report significant differences on several "need" dimensions, tested through the Edwards Personal Preference Schedule. Specifically, the career group scored higher on the Achievement, Intraception and Endurance scales, while the home group scored significantly higher on the Succorance and Heterosexuality scales, suggesting that these needs reflect motivations that lead women in either the career- or home-oriented direction.

Rand (1968) examined the hypothesis that career-oriented college women possess more traditionally masculine characteristics (including the need for achievement, dominance, endurance, independence, competency and recognition), while homemaking-oriented women reflect more traditional feminine characteristics (nurturance, succorance, empathy, understanding and sociability). The homemaking sample consisted of those women who agreed that "finding a husband in college was more important than finding a suitable field of training" while the career sample disagreed with this statement and expected to obtain advanced degrees (M.D., J.D., D.D.S. or Ph.D.). Testing of these two extreme groups confirmed the hypothesis and it was concluded that career-oriented women had expanded their roles to include behaviors characteristic of both sexes while the homemaking-oriented women adhered to the traditional feminine role.

These studies and others (Barnett, 1971; Gysbers, et al., 1968; Masih, 1967) have established that need for achievement tends to be stronger in career-oriented women while a more salient need for affiliation or nurturance is typical of homemaking-oriented women. This is consistent with the thesis that identification with the traditional feminine role may result from either a low need for achievement or a high need for affiliation while the reverse would be true of women who are career-oriented (Bardwick and Douwan, 1971). Oliver (1974), in an empirical investigation of this hypothesis, found a significant interaction between achievement and affiliation motivation in college women.

Locus of control has also been hypothesized to be a determinant of career orientation, but data related to this has been inconsistent. Maracek and Frasch (1977) reported that the college women in their study who exhibited higher internal orientations showed greater career commitment, expected to work longer, engaged in more career planning, and felt less discomfort about violating sex-role stereotypes than women with external orientations. Parsons, et al. (1978), on the other hand, point out that when a group faces societal opposition (as women aspiring to high-level careers often do), an external orientation which assumes less personal failure might lead to higher self-esteem and an increased desire to assume nontraditional roles. Their data support this hypothesis.

Stewart and Winter (1974) hypothesized that the differences between women undergraduates planning a continuous career involvement and those who were primarily marriage and family oriented related to a self-definition versus social-definition dimension. Career-oriented women would tend to exhibit a pattern of self-definition, freer from ascriptive demands. On a projective storytelling measure, they found that these women "organized their perceptions in terms of causality, purpose and instrumentality, as opposed to irrational diffusion . . . they tended to engage in instrumental behavior more often than socially defined women and admit to behavior which is negatively sanctioned for women" (p. 257). The authors felt that those patterns appeared systematically from verbal expression through social and political behavior and were "not merely patterns of career choice or career salience but coherent personality patterns or styles" (p. 259).

Attitudinal Variables

Attitudinal factors, particularly sex-role attitudes, have been shown to relate to career orientations. It has been suggested that society, by use of subtle techniques of social influence, trains women to accept the traditional roles ascribed to them (Bem and Bem, 1970). To the extent that a young woman has accepted this ideology and has traditional attitudes toward the role of women she will be less career-oriented. Studies have indeed supported the hypothesis that career aspirations and commitment among college women are related to their sex-role attitudes (Bielby, 1978; Friedman, 1976; Hawley, 1969; Zuckerman, 1978). In fact, in a study by Parsons, et. al. (1978), investigating a variety of socialization, situational, attitudinal and personality variables, attitudinal factors were found to best predict career aspirations, accounting for 27 percent of the total variance.

Frankel (1974) hypothesized that sex-role attitudes are important in that they act to encourage or inhibit positive self-concept and achievement- or goal-oriented behavior. Those women who accept the traditional attitudes regarding femininity and appropriate sex-role behavior, i.e., that femininity implies passive, dependent behavior, are likely to attempt to conform to this view and will therefore be less actively achievement-oriented than women who reject this ideology. Results of her study support this hypothesis. Similarly, Hjelle and Butterfield (1974) indicate that women with pro-feminist attitudes exhibit greater self-actualization.

Weathers (1979) proposed that perceiving a high degree of potential for borrowing prestige from one's husband would lessen motivation for a woman's own vocational achievement. Data confirmed that high and low career commitment groups differed in their perceptions of prestige borrowing.

Attitudes toward combining dual roles are important. Barnett (1971) found that women with consistent career-oriented attitudes anticipated no difficulty in combining roles and expected to do so while women who were less career-oriented were ambivalent about combining roles and anticipated many problems in any attempts to integrate a career and a family. This latter group expected that they would quickly abandon any vocational plans if opposed by parents or prospective mates.

Hawley (1971) has shown that anticipated role-behavior of women is strongly affected by their perception of the male's stereotype of women, regardless of the actual stereotypes men may hold. Other studies have also considered perceptions about the attitudes of peers or other significant persons to be a relevant factor (Barnett, 1971; Matthews and Tiedeman, 1964; Parsons, et al., 1978).

The type of motivation for work, or work values, also may vary. Simpson and Simpson (1961) found that career-oriented college women more often stressed intrinsic features of work while non-career-oriented subjects stressed extrinsic features. Richardson (1974) reports similar results. She tested college women on a wide variety of measures and found that the pattern of relationships among the variables formed two major clusters. The first she defined as career orientation. Career-oriented women were highly motivated, perceived their career roles as being primary in their lives and sought intrinsic satisfaction from work. The second cluster, work orientation, characterized women who valued both career and family roles, but with the latter taking clear priority. These women were more likely to choose traditionally feminine occupations and were motivated by both intrinsic and extrinsic rewards.

Summary

The research data reviewed has shown that career-oriented college women differ from homemaking-oriented subjects on a number of variables. While the data are not conclusive, career-oriented women seem more likely to have come from middle-class families where the mother was employed and to have parents who value academic achievement over more traditional feminine attributes such as appearance. In general, these women have less traditional attitudes toward sex roles and are likely to feel they can successfully integrate home and career roles. Career-oriented women also tend more to have incorporated traditional masculine traits, such as achievement and independence, into their self-definitions.

There are methodological problems with the data, though, that make generalizations difficult. First, nearly every study uses a different definition to categorize subjects into groups. Some take only women who fall into one of the extremes and exclude those women who expect to have dual roles. Those studies that do include this latter group differ on whether they belong to the career-oriented or family-oriented subset. Dichotomizing college women into only two categories is problematic in itself as these categories are extremely broad. A number of investigators, for instance, have looked at smaller groups, especially exploring differences between women preparing for traditional as opposed to nontraditional women's careers (Almquist and Angrist, 1970; Mintz and Patterson, 1969; Trigg and Perlman, 1976).

In addition, as noted earlier, it is not known to what extent the subjects used in these studies will actually implement their plans. Angrist (1972) in a longitudinal study of college women found that almost half changed their orientations at least once during their college years alone. Baruch (1972) suggests that the career issue is a salient one during college but changes later when realistic considerations of husband and family become more important. There is some empirical evidence that career salience declines after marriage especially during the childrearing years (Bielby, 1978). On the other hand, it has been suggested that women tend to idealize marriage and motherhood while they are single and that career salience increases after childbearing. Travis (1976), for example, found that women without children were especially likely to believe that motherhood is incompatible with a career. These contradictory theories and data illustrate the difficulty in assuming that career orientation either remains stable over time or changes in a predictable pattern.

Chapter Summary and Discussion

The literature review has focused on a variety of topics related to the orientation of women toward work and family roles. A number of significant points have emerged which will be briefly reiterated and discussed.

It is apparent that labor force participation by married women has increased substantially since World War II. A number of social and economic factors—including decreasing birth rate, expanding economy, increased educational level of women, technological changes and the recent inflation—have contributed to these changes and suggest that the increasing participation of women in paid employment will continue. Further, they have been accompanied by changes in attitudes such that the dual roles of motherhood and career are no longer considered rare or abnormal. Evidence indicates that many women, if not most, want to play a role in both the domestic and occupational spheres and expect to be able to do so.

However, upon closer examination it becomes clear that these attitudinal and statistical changes—while quite real—are not nearly as dramatic as many investigators suggest. When the statistics relating to women with children, especially preschool children, are reviewed, the percentage of women who continue their careers full-time (as most men do) during the childrearing years is seen to be surprisingly low. Only about 10 percent of women with children under six have continuous full-time involvement in the labor force. This number is probably higher for those with greater education.

Likewise, attitudes toward working mothers and the role of women in general have not, in this investigator's opinion, undergone the massive change that has often been portrayed. True, it is quite acceptable for women to work because of critical financial need, but this has always been the case. It has also become more acceptable for women to work for "personal satisfaction" when their children are older. However, it does not seem to be considered appropriate for women to work for personal reasons when they have small children (although some conclude otherwise), and it is rare for a woman to give equal status, let alone priority, to her career. There is little evidence to suggest that the traditional ideology has abandoned its major assumptions, although they do seem to have been revised. In fact, it appears that in earlier studies, somewhere around 20 percent accepted the idea of dual roles for women; in recent investigations, about the same number accept the idea of continuous dual involvement for women by choice.

Thus, although dual roles for women are endorsed in the abstract, in reality they are neither totally approved nor easily managed. Studies of families in which both husband and wife maintain career involvement attest to the many difficulties existing for women who attempt this lifestyle. Further, they illustrate that the problem originates not only from societal pressures but, perhaps more importantly, from internal pressures. The women themselves, although generally highly educated, have internalized traditional norms and have set up standards for themselves which interfere with the realization of their full career potential. It is important to remember, of course, that these women do not feel dissatisfied with their situation in general but feel they have the best of both worlds. It is possible, though, that the conflict between roles is felt more acutely by young women today who have been exposed to fluctuating ideologies.

While there is thus contradictory evidence and differing interpretations of the degree to which changes have occurred, the fact remains that millions of women are employed today, even when they have young children at home. Retrospective studies indicate that the majority do so for economic reasons and certainly, given the state of today's economy, this is a critical factor. However, other elements are clearly involved (including interests outside the home, achievement needs and dissatisfaction with homemaking), although they may be considered secondary by most subjects. It was posited that a combination of factors need to be investigated to determine the relative benefits and costs to the individual; that is, one factor alone, even financial concerns, may not be enough to motivate a woman to work if other advantages are not also perceived or if the cost (such as perception of harm to the child) is too great.

Studies comparing working and nonworking women, as well as career-oriented and homemaking-oriented college women, suggest that there may be substantial differences in background, personality and attitudinal variables between these groups. Women who work, or plan to work, tend to have had families which emphasized achievement, to have higher self-esteem and greater achievement needs, to have different types of interests and to have more liberal attitudes toward the role of women when compared to those who are, or expect to be, primarily homemakers.

As has been pointed out, however, this area of research has been lacking in methodological controls. Widely varying, heterogeneous groups have been studied and a number of confounding variables introduced that lead to ambiguous results. Women are studied either after they have been engaged in their roles for some time or years prior to the point at which a decision needs to be made. Thus it is unclear what factors actually differentiate various populations of women who plan varying combinations of roles. In addition, since this area may be undergoing rapid change, it is unclear how young women today feel about this issue. What is needed are investigations of women in similar circumstances at the point when they are actually making their plans. This is what the present study aims to do.

Thus, we are interested in learning what factors differentiate women who interrupt their careers at childbirth from those who plan to maintain dual role involvement. Further, we hope to gain insight into motivations behind this decision and the process by which plans are made. How do women today approach this issue, what factors or combination of factors are most salient and how much have changing norms affected them?

3

Methods

This study investigates factors related to women's plans to continue or interrupt their careers at the birth of their first child. Questionnaires were given to women and their husbands who were attending Lamaze classes prior to the child's birth. The couples were then placed in one of three groups and compared on a range of demographic, personality and attitudinal variables.

Population to Be Studied

The population investigated was composed of women (and their husbands) who were expecting their first child. The first pregnancy was chosen because it was felt that this is the time when the issues surrounding motherhood and career roles become most salient. By the time of childbirth, most women need to have made initial decisions regarding whether or not they expect to return to paid employment after the baby is born, although it is certainly possible that they may alter their plans later. However, it was felt that initial plans made is an important area of study, as well as providing methodological control, since all subjects are studied at the same point.

Three specific alternative options commonly chosen by women today were selected for study. These were: (1) Full-time Employment—planning to work full-time within six months after childbirth, (2) Part-time Employment—planning to begin part-time employment within six months after childbirth, and (3) Full-time Homemaker—planning no employment for at least one and one-half years after childbirth.

The first and third options (i.e. full-time employment and full-time homemaking) are clearly the two alternatives most often discussed in the literature and seem to be the most common alternatives for women today. Generally, part-time employment is considered as part of the former since it reflects a commitment to continuing one's career. However, it was felt that women who plan this option may constitute a distinct group. A study by Hall and Gordon (1973) supports this hypothesis. They examined conflict and satisfaction among the three groups mentioned above and found that "the difference between part-time and full-time work is as distinct as that between working and not working" (p. 47). They suggest that a woman who works part-time may be a different type of person altogether from a woman in the other two groups.

The study compared married women in these three groups, as well as their husbands. Although the major focus was on the women themselves, it was felt that husbands may have an important influence on their wives' plans. Those studies of husbands that have been reported suggest that there are significant differences between husbands of women who work and husbands of women who are not employed. Therefore, they were included in this investigation.

Sampling Criteria

To be included in the final sample, women had to meet the following criteria. They had to be: (1) Caucasian, (2) between the ages of 22 and 40, (3) married and currently living with their husbands, (4) pregnant with their first child, (5) attending Lamaze classes, (6) working full-time at the time when they became pregnant, (7) a college graduate (4 year degree), and (8) in a professional, technical or managerial occupation as defined in the Dictionary of Occupational Titles (U.S. Dept. of Labor, 1977).

These criteria were imposed in an effort to control for some of the more obvious potential confounding variables. For example, women who are not married, have less than a college education or are working in low status jobs would tend, as a group, to be more likely to work because of critical financial need and might also be less career-oriented. It was expected that choosing women in similar situations, with relatively comparable educations, at the same stage in the family cycle would avoid some of the methodological difficulties noted in previous studies.

Procedures

Pilot Study

A pilot study was undertaken prior to initiation of the final investigation in an effort to determine the feasibility of the study, refine procedures and test the questionnaire.

Initially it was proposed that potential subjects be recruited from a variety of sources, including Lamaze classes, obstetricians' offices and childbirth preparation classes. In anticipation of this, two groups of obstetricians were contacted and permission was sought to post notices in their offices soliciting participants. Permission was given by both groups and notices were posted. However, it was later decided that this procedure involved too many uncontrolled variables; for example, there was no way of reliably knowing how many potential subjects did not respond and if volunteers thus comprised a narrow group which was systematically different from the more general population. Therefore, it was decided that subjects should be recruited exclusively from Lamaze classes.

The administrator of NIASPO, the parent organization that oversees Lamaze classes in the Chicago area, was contacted during the pilot phase and, after having the study explained, recommended a Lamaze instructor whom she thought would be helpful. This instructor agreed to cooperate by allowing the investigator to attend one of her classes and recruit potential subjects. She also suggested two other instructors, who likewise agreed. A total of five classes were attended during the pilot phase.

As a result of this experience, the procedures were modified and the questionnaire revised. Initially, interested couples were asked to submit their names and addresses and the questionnaires were mailed to them. This proved problematic as there was no indication of why some couples agreed to participate while others refused. In addition, only a small number of couples actually returned the questionnaires.

A new procedure was then tried. Each couple in the class was asked to complete an information sheet even if they did not choose to participate. Those who did agree were given questionnaires immediately and asked to return them to the investigator at the next class.

This procedure was utilized for the final study for several reasons. The information sheet made it possible to measure participation rates and to assess whether there were any gross differences between couples who agreed to participate and those who refused. In addition, the response rate of participating couples greatly improved—presumably by tying the questionnaire to the class. In addition, since the investigator would personally collect the completed data, there was some motivation to return the questionnaires as the couples had already agreed to participate. Having the questionnaires returned the next week also allowed the investigator to quickly ascertain how many more subjects needed to be recruited. Besides these advantages for the investigator, it was felt that this procedure afforded the subjects increased confidentiality by making it no longer necessary for them to indicate their names and addresses.

The pilot study served several other purposes as well. The high percentage of couples who agreed to participate and their personal reactions made it clear that this was a topic of interest and that it was a feasible study to conduct. Subjects in the pilot study were also asked to give their reactions to the questionnaire. While responses varied, the majority found the survey interesting and often used it to initiate discussion with their spouses concering this issue. As a result of suggestions and responses to questions, some questions were eliminated or reworded and a few questions added. It was also felt by many subjects that the questionnaire was longer than they had expected. While little was done to change this, the investigator did include in her initial presentation the fact that the questionnaire was lengthy.

The pilot study, while dispelling some of the initial concerns about the feasibility of the study (e.g., that husbands might not respond), did point up a significant difficulty with the initial subject-requirements. The original study called for subjects who were highly educated (i.e., had graduate degrees) and in nontraditional women's fields (e.g., medicine, law, business). However, results of the pilot study indicated that this was unrealistic; while many of the potential subjects had college educations, only a small percentage had advanced degrees and an even fewer number were in nontraditional fields. Thus it was decided to include in the sample all women with a minimum of a four-year college degree who were in professional, technical or managerial positions.

Preliminary Steps

Before the final study took place, several preliminary steps, in addition to the pilot study, were taken.

An application to conduct the study was submitted to the Northwestern University Human Subjects Review committee and was approved.

The President and the Administrator of NIASPO were contacted and asked for permission to recruit participants from Lamaze classes. A proposal was sent to them and the NIASPO Board of Directors granted the investigator permission to contact individual teachers, with the stipulation that it would be the individual instructor's decision whether or not to allow members of their class to be recruited.

The President of NIASPO announced in one of their monthly meetings that teachers were being sought who would cooperate in the study. Seven teachers from Chicago and surrounding suburbs agreed to participate. In addition, nine instructors had already been referred by their colleagues. After being contacted and told about the study, seven of these agreed to cooperate. The other two had a general policy of not allowing individuals to approach members of their class for any reason whatsoever. Thus a total of fourteen instructors (each of whom conducted one or two classes a week) allowed the investigator to speak to their classes about the study and ask for volunteers.

Final Procedures

All subjects included in the final sample were contacted through Lamaze classes in prepared childbirth. Each class is taught by an individual, trained instructor (usually an R. N.) and runs for six weeks. Both women and their husbands generally attend in the third trimester of pregnancy and there is normally a fee charged.

With the prior approval of the instructor, the investigator attended one of the classes in a series to recruit participants. The third, fourth or fifth class was chosen, depending on the instructor's preferences and the investigator's schedule.

At the class, the instructor introduced the investigator and generally explained briefly that she was there to tell the couples about a research project. This introduction varied in length and detail depending on the instructor.

The investigator then spoke for approximately five minutes, explaining who she was, details of the study and what participation would require. Specifically, it was explained to couples that:

a) The investigator was a graduate student in clinical psychology at Northwestern University and was conducting a study for her dissertation.
b) The study would be looking at some of the factors that might be involved in a woman's decision to interrupt or continue her career at the birth of her first child; i.e., why some women choose one alternative while others choose another.
c) Participants for the study—couples who were having their first child, in which the woman has been involved in a career—were being sought.
d) Participation in the study would require that each spouse complete a questionnaire that asked about their future plans regarding employment, factors involved in these plans, attitudes about male and female roles in society and their personality characteristics.
e) Questionnaires would be given to those willing to participate and collected by the investigator at the following class meeting.
f) Participation was completely voluntary.
g) Responses would be strictly confidential and data analyzed in terms of groups, not individuals.

Questions from members of the class were then solicited and answered. Following this, the investigator distributed a one-page information sheet (see Appendix A) to each couple in the class, asking for the husband's and wife's level of education, their occupations and the wife's plans regarding employment after the baby's birth. This information was to be used to determine the general population from which the sample was drawn and the rate of response. The information sheet also asked whether or not the couple was willing to participate in the study. Those persons who agreed to participate were asked to read and sign a consent form.

At that point, each member of the class (both husband and wife) who had agreed to participate was given a questionnaire in a manila envelope. They were reminded again that the questionnaires would be collected by the investigator at the next meeting and encouraged to complete them.

At the next class meeting (one week later), questionnaires were collected. Those individuals who did not return them at that time were given a stamped, addressed envelope and asked to return the questionnaire by mail as soon as possible.

In a few cases, questionnaires were collected the next week by the instructor. This was due either to the instructor's preference or to the unavailability of the investigator.

A total of 25 classes were attended. Twelve of these were in Chicago; the other 13 in the suburbs. Of the 194 couples in these classes, 159 agreed to participate. Sixteen women were expecting their second child; another ten had not worked for many years or otherwise felt the study was inappropriate to their situation. Thus, only nine couples actually declined to participate in the study, with 95 percent of potential subjects agreeing to cooperate.

Of the couples who agreed to participate, 95 of the women had a minimum of a college degree, were engaged in a professional, technical or managerial occupation and otherwise met the requirements of the study. While questionnaires were given to and collected from couples who did not meet these requirements, these subjects were not included in the final data analysis.

Seventy-eight of the couples meeting all criteria returned questionnaires. In three additional cases, only the husbands returned the questionnaires, but these were not included in the analysis (or in the response rate). Thus the response rate was 78 percent, with no significant differences across groups (χ^2 = .36, 2 d.f., n.s.).

Instruments

Several instruments were selected for inclusion in the questionnaire completed by each subject, as well as single items used by other researchers or developed by the investigator. The following is a description of the measures used. A sample of both questionnaires (wives and husbands) may be found in Appendix B.

Personality Research Form (PRF)

The review of the literature, as well as intuitive reasoning, led to the hypothesis that personality needs (in particular, need for achievement and need for nurturance) might be related to the plans women made regarding employment.

The PRF (Jackson, 1974) was used to assess eight personality variables that were thought to be particularly relevant. The needs measured were: Achievement, Affiliation, Autonomy, Change, Dominance, Nurturance, Social Recognition and Succorance. Designed as a self-report personality inventory for use within the normal range, the PRF-Form E measures each trait by means of a 16 item scale.

The inventory was chosen for several reasons. Besides the fact that it assesses the personality variables of interest in a nonpsychiatric population and is easily administered and scored, the scales were developed both on the basis of a theoretical framework (Henry Murray's personality theory) as well as extensive empirical analysis. The reliability and validity of the inventory have been examined extensively, with generally positive results. In addition, the PRF has been found to be useful in a number of research studies, with a range of populations (Jackson, 1974). Thus, it appeared to be a relatively sophisticated, as well as relevant, instrument.

Sex-Role Attitude Scale

It seemed likely that sex-role attitudes would also be a particularly relevant factor associated with the women's employment plans. To measure these attitudes, a scale was derived from several component scales that reflected varying aspects of sex-role attitudes. The following scales were included.

The Osmond-Martin Sex-Role Attitudes Scale. Developed by Osmond and Martin (1975), the Sex-Role Attitudes Scale (SRA) is a thirty-one-item Likert Scale intended to tap several components of sex roles. The modern (liberal) versus traditional (conservative) continuum that it reflects incorporates two conceptualizations, equality versus inequality and sex differentiation versus nontyping of social roles on the basis of sex. "'Traditional' sex-roles are those which are based on polar, dichotomous conceptions of the nature and roles of men versus women [while] 'modern' roles ... are characterized by flexible and dynamic transcendence of sex-role constraints; that is, 'modern' definitions of social roles are not specified by 'sex'" (Osmond and Martin, 1975, p. 1).

The scale, while measuring a single dimension (of modern to traditional), is designed to tap attitudes in four component areas. These are: (1) familial roles of males and females, (2) extrafamilial roles of each sex, (3) stereotypes of male/female characteristics and behaviors and (4) social change as related to sex roles.

Preliminary reliability and validity studies have been reported (Osmond and Martin, 1975). Although this scale has not been used as extensively as others, it was chosen primarily for three reasons. One, it was felt that the items were more up-to-date than earlier scales. Second, the scale was conceptualization of a sex-role continuum as one which involves lesser or greater degrees of sex differentiation and typing. Thus, items tapping social roles of both sexes are included, although the primary focus quantitatively is still women. Third, the scale was developed to tap component areas, thus making it possible to assess attitudes toward sex roles in a variety of contexts.

Attitudes Toward Dual Roles of Married Professional Women. This is a six-item questionnaire devised by Kaley (1971) to tap attitudes toward the dual role of married, professional women. The emphasis concerns whether mothers who attempt to perform dual roles (career and homemaking) can fulfill family obligations as well as full-time homemakers. Reliability and validity studies are not reported; however, the use of the scale in research studies (Etaugh, 1973; Kaley, 1971) attests in part to its utility. The scale was included in the present study to assess whether subjects felt it was possible for a woman to have a career without harming her family.

Attitudes toward motherhood. Six items tapping attitudes toward motherhood (Lieberman, Reibstein and Sweny, 1979) were included to assess subjects' attitudes and biases toward mothers.

The composite scale, including the Osmond-Martin sex-role attitude scale with its four component subscales, Kaley's items regarding dual roles of professional women, and the items assessing attitudes toward motherhood, was administered to all subjects. Because of the lack of adequate reliability studies of these measures, the degree of internal consistency (i.e., the degree to which each scale measured a uniform dimension) was evaluated. In addition, this provided a means of evaluating whether these scales could be used to form one major scale, as well as the six subscales.

Reliability coefficients, measured by Cronbach's alpha, were computed for each scale and items deleted which substantially lowered the reliability. The recalculated alphas are shown in Table 3-1. The coefficients for both the total scale and the revised Osmond-Martin scale were .84, reflecting a high reliability. However, the coefficients for the subscales were lower, ranging from .59 to .80. Although still within acceptable limits, they indicate that caution is called for in interpreting results.

Intrinsic and Extrinsic Motivation Scales

Derived from standard job assessment questions used by the Survey Research Center, the University of Michigan, and revised by Graef, Csikszentmihalyi and Griffin (1978), these Likert scales are designed to measure the importance of intrinsic and extrinsic job components. Extrinsic

Table 3–1.   Reliability Coefficients of Sex-Role Attitude Scales

Scale	Reliability Coefficient Alpha
Total SRA Scale	.84
Revised Osmond-Martin Scale	.84
Familial Roles	.59
Extrafamilial Roles	.65
Stereotypes	.61
Need for Social Change	.70
Dual Roles Scale	.80
Value of Motherhood	.63

rewards are those outcomes that are controlled by the employer, including salary, security and formal recognition, while intrinsic rewards refer to rewards that the individual, in effect, bestows on himself such as feelings of accomplishment. The scales were developed theoretically, based on the distinction between the two general types of rewards. They were included to assess subjects' work-related motivations.

Questionnaire

A questionnaire was developed by the investigator which incorporated the above mentioned scales as well as additional items deemed relevant to the issue being studied. The following sets of variables were included:

Demographic information. These variables include age, marital status, religion, education and occupational factors.

Decision-making process. These items include future employment plans, certainty of plans, who was involved in the decision, and feelings about the plans made.

Conscious motivations for plans. Subjects were asked to indicate and to rank the importance of a list of factors to their decision.

Perceptions of roles. These items reflect the absolute and relative importance to their identities of work, family and personal roles and were modelled after questions used by Hall and Hall (1979) and Bailyn (1970).

Husband's support. These two items assess the husband's attitude toward and support for his wife's career. They were modelled after categorizations used by Garland (1972).

Attitudes. In addition to the sex-role attitude scales described above, questions regarding subjects' attitudes and behaviors regarding responsibility for household tasks and childcare were included. Such types of questions are frequently asked in research concerning family roles (Nye, 1976; Salo, 1977).

Subjects

Data was collected from 78 couples (70 of which fit one of the three groups), all volunteers from Lamaze classes in the greater Chicago Metropolitan area. All of the women were white, married, and currently living with their husbands. Each was in her third trimester of pregnancy and expecting her first child. All had worked full-time and were in professional, technical or managerial occupations. The occupations represented by the women in the sample are listed in Table 3-2.

The ages of the women in the sample ranged from 23 to 38 with a mean age of 28.9 and a mode of 29. The mean age of the men was 31.1 and ranged from 24 to 50; their modal age was 29.

This was the first marriage for 92 percent of the couples; 8 percent had been married previously. The subjects had been married an average length of 3.5 years, varying from two months to twelve years.

Of the women in the sample, 24.4 percent were Protestant, 37.2 percent Catholic and 24.4 percent Jewish, with 14 percent listing no religious affiliation. Twenty-seven percent of the men indicated they were Protestant, 37.2 percent Catholic and 20.5 percent Jewish. No affiliation was listed by 15.4 percent of the men.

All of the women had at least a bachelor's degree; 47 percent had some graduate training as well. The average length of formal education was 17 years. There was no minimum education requirement for the husbands; however, all but six of the men (7.7 percent) had college degrees and 58 percent had some graduate training. Their average length of education was 17.1 years.

The women had been working an average of 5.4 years, varying from one to fifteen years. They earned an average of $16,600, ranging from $1,000 to $42,000. At the time of the survey, 94 percent of the husbands were working full-time; another 2.6 percent part-time. They had been working an average of 6.5 years, with a range of 1 to 28, and were earning up to $100,000, with a mean income of $30,000.

Thus, educational level, occupational status and earned income places these couples in the middle and upper socioeconomic strata.

Table 3–2.   Women's Occupations Represented

3 Accountant	1 Microbiologist
3 Advertising Executive	6 Nurse
3 Administrator	2 Nutrition Consultant
2 Audiologist	1 Occupational Therapist
6 Business Manager	1 Physician
2 College Professor	1 Psychologist
5 Commercial Artist	1 Public Relations Consultant
4 Computer Programmer	1 Rehabilitation Counselor
1 Editor	1 Speech Pathologist
2 Interior Designer	3 Social Worker
5 Lawyer	17 Teacher
1 Librarian	1 Television Director
2 Management Consultant	1 Writer
2 Marketing Manager	

In regard to the pregnancy itself, 72 percent of the women (and 67 percent of their husbands) indicated that the pregnancy was planned; 27 percent and 30 percent, respectively, said that it was not. The women wanted to have anywhere from one to five children, averaging 2.3, while the men ranged from one to nine and averaged 2.4.

Of the total sample of 78, 23 (29.5 percent) of the women planned to return to work full-time within six months; 21 (26.9 percent) planned to begin working on a part-time basis within six months, and 26 (33.4 percent) planned no paid employment for at least one and one-half years. Eight of the women (10.3 percent) indicated that they were undecided about their future employment plans at the point the survey was taken. These women were not included in the analyses of group differences that comprise the major portion of this study.

In comparison to their wives, 95 percent of the men planned to work full-time after the birth of their baby. Two of the men (2.6 percent) planned to work part-time, while two planned no outside employment in the immediate future. These four were all in full-time graduate programs.

Data Analysis

The major research question was: What factors are associated with a woman's plans to interrupt or continue her career after the birth of her first child?

The strategy used in the investigation was to compare subjects on a variety of variables, including personality characteristics, sex-role attitudes and husband's support. The decision-making process, motivational factors and perception of roles were also investigated. These variables were chosen on the basis of prior research and their perceived relevancy to the present study.

Subjects were placed in one of three groups, depending upon the woman's future plans. Twenty-three of the women, the Full-time Group, expected to return to full-time employment within six months after the birth of the baby. Twenty-one women, the Part-time Group, expected to begin working part-time within the same period of time. The Home Group was comprised of twenty-six women who did not plan to return to paid employment for at least one and one-half years, if not longer. The eight women who were undecided regarding their future employment plans were excluded from the final analyses. Husbands were placed in the same groups as their wives; for example, husbands whose wives planned to work part-time were placed in the Part-time Group.

One-way analyses of variance were used to determine differences among these groups for the majority of variables. Post hoc comparisons of all possible pairings of groups were then made, using Duncan's Multiple Range Test (with the alpha level set at .05). Tables report the results of this latter comparison by indicating which groups have significantly higher or lower means. For example, F, P>H indicates that both the Full-time and Part-time groups were significantly higher on that variable than the Home Group and that there is no significant difference between the Full-time and Part-time Groups. F>H would indicate that the Full-time Group is significantly higher on the variable than the Home Group but that the Part-time Group is not significantly different on this variable compared to either of the other two groups.

A small percentage of variables did not meet the assumption of equal variances needed to validly employ the F test. Since analysis of variance is relatively robust with regard to violations of this assumption, it was not viewed as a serious problem. However, as a further check, the Kruskal-Wallis test (and, when appropriate, the Median Test) were used to test differences among groups on these variables. In no instance was the result changed; that is, variables which showed a significant difference among groups remained significant and variables which did not originally differentiate groups remained nonsignificant. Since the results did not vary, for the sake of consistency and because of the use of the post hoc comparisons, the F test is reported throughout.

Further, ANOVA is reported for data ranked by the subjects (e.g., rank order of motivational factors) despite the fact that assumptions of independence are violated. However, it was felt that reporting the results of this statistical test would prove useful in understanding the data. Further, there is some support for the use of ANOVA statistics even with rank-order data (Kerlinger, 1973).

The Chi-square test was the statistic used to evaluate categorical data.

In some cases, where analysis of variance was initially used, the results are reported in the form of a contingency table to facilitate comprehension of the data. In these instances, the chi-square test was then employed and these results reported. Again, however, the two statistical analyses showed consistent results.

It should also be noted that, on occasion, some subjects did not respond to a particular question. Therefore, the actual N is, at times, less than 70. However, the number of missing values, unless otherwise noted, is less than 10 percent, and for the sake of clarity not given for each separate variable.

4

Results and Discussion

This chapter describes the results of the study and offers some preliminary interpretations. The major portion of this section examines whether any of the variables tested differentiate among the three groups. A secondary exploration of subsets within the Full-time Group follows. Finally, combinations of variables will be examined to determine which best accounts for the variations among the groups.

Demographic Characteristics

Characteristics of the sample, as a whole, have been described in the previous section. Comparisons were also made to determine whether or not there were any significant differences among the three groups. These results, reported in Table 4-1, indicate that there were no significant differences among the three groups in age, years of marriage, husband's education or husband's income. Neither were there significant differences in religion, marital status or marital satisfaction.

There is, however, a significant difference in the mean educational level of the women in the three groups, despite the fact that all had a minimum of a college education. In the Home Group, only 27 percent had gone beyond this level of formal education, while in the Full-time Group, 70 percent had at least one year of graduate training. There was greater variability in the Part-time Group, with approximately half (52 percent) of the women having had some graduate training. Statistically, this group was more similar to the Home Group in educational level, according to Duncan's Multiple Range Test.

The finding that women with greater education are more likely to work is consistent with national data (U.S. Department of Commerce, 1979). Although the present study is correlational in nature, one might speculate on the causal relationship between these variables. It is possible, for example, that obtaining graduate education may lead a woman to plan to continue her career by changing her attitudes or enabling her to be in a more satisfying

Table 4–1. Demographic Characteristics

Variable	Full-time (N=23) Mean	Part-time (N=21) Mean	Home (N=26) Mean	F	Duncan's Test
Age					
Women	29.8	28.6	28.5	1.11	
Men	31.4	31.3	31.0	.04	
Years Married	3.2	3.5	3.3	.05	
Education (in years)					
Women	17.7	16.9	16.4	9.33**	F > P,H
Men	17.5	16.9	16.9	.96	
Income (in thousands)					
Women	19.6	16.3	14.0	3.10*	F > P,H
Men	24.3	35.8	33.8	2.46	

*$p < .06$.
**$p < .001$.

position. On the other hand, one might hypothesize that those women who want to work during most of their adult years are more likely to seek higher education in order to advance their careers. While both theories have validity, there is a great deal of research to support the latter conclusion. Studies indicate that college women who are more career-oriented plan to pursue more education and tend to do so (Angrist, 1966; Gyspers, Johnston and Gust, 1968; Watley and Kaplan, 1971). Thus, obtaining graduate education may be a reflection of the same factors that lead a woman to continue her career investment even when she has young children.

Differences in the mean income of women in the three groups approaches statistical significance. Women in the Full-time Group tend to have higher earnings from their most recent jobs. This finding would seem to be related to the higher educational levels achieved; i.e., higher status and higher salaries are generally correlated with education. In fact, with education controlled, this difference no longer approaches significance ($F = 2.05$, $p = .137$).

Perhaps even more noteworthy, however, and difficult to ignore, is the fact that women in the Full-time Group tend to earn a higher percentage of the total family income. On the average, these women earn 46 percent of the family income while women in the Part-time and Home groups contribute 35 percent and 31 percent, respectively ($F = 5.38$, $p < .01$). This suggests that women who have substantial incomes, particularly if their incomes contribute a high percent of the total family income, may find it more difficult to give up their jobs.

Thus, except for wife's education and income, the couples in all three groups are similar in regard to demographic variables.

Occupational Characteristics

While a wide range of occupations were represented in the sample (See Table 3-2), all of the women were in professional, technical or managerial positions, as categorized by the Dictionary of Occupational Titles (U.S. Department of Labor, 1977). However, to determine variations within this grouping, two measures were utilized.

The first was a measure of occupational prestige (National Opinion Research Center, 1974). Results (Table 4-2) indicate that the occupations of women in the Full-time Group were more prestigious than those of women in either the Part-time or Home Groups. This is not surprising since occupational prestige is highly correlated with the educational background necessary for employment in that field (National Opinion Research Center, 1974). Again, when education is controlled for, the differences in prestige are no longer significant (F = 2.37, p = .103).

Occupations were also classified depending on their traditionality for women. Occupations in which more than 75 percent of those employed are women were considered traditional while those with less than 25 percent women were categorized as pioneer. Other occupations were classified as moderate (U.S. Department of Labor, 1977). Although studies have found that women in pioneer occupations are more career-oriented than women in traditional fields (Nagely, 1971; Wolkon, 1972), differences among the three groups in this sample were not significant (Table 4-3).

Women in all three groups had been working in their occupations an average of five to six years (Table 4-2) and there were no differences in reported satisfaction; the majority in all groups reported being very or somewhat satisfied about their careers.

Intrinsic and extrinsic motivations for work were measured (Table 4-2) and no differences found among groups, despite studies which suggest that intrinsic rewards are of greater value to career women (Turner, 1964; Wolkon, 1972).

The amount of time spent working before pregnancy did not vary among groups (Table 4-2); however, perceived flexibility did (Table 4-2). Women in the Part-time Group reported having jobs with the greatest flexibility. This, no doubt, contributed to their ability to work part-time, if desired, whereas more women in the other groups may have been forced to choose between working full-time or quitting.

Thus, differences in occupational characteristics among women in the

Table 4–2.   Occupational Characteristics

Variable	Full-time (N=23) Mean	Part-time (N=21) Mean	Home (N=26) Mean	F	Duncan's Test
Prestige Scores					
Women	65.1	57.2	57.3	5.76**	F > H,P
Men	61.7	53.5	57.5	2.52	
Years in Occupation					
Women	6.1	5.7	4.7	1.46	
Men	5.8	8.0	6.0	1.44	
Job Flexibility					
Women	3.5	2.7	3.6	3.12*	P > F,H
Men	3.4	3.0	3.3	.48	
Intrinsic Motivation Score[a]					
Women	35.3	35.8	35.6	.06	
Men	35.4	30.1	34.5	2.25	
Extrinsic Motivation Score[b]					
Women	39.9	38.2	39.5	.28	
Men	41.3	36.6	39.1	1.64	

[a] Intrinsic scores may range from 6 (low) to 42 (high).
[b] Extrinsic scores may range from 8 (low) to 56 (high).
* $p < .05$.
** $p < .01$.

Table 4–3.   Percentage of Women in Traditional Occupations

	Full-time (N=23)	Part-time (N=21)	Home (N=26)	χ^2
Traditional	46%	35%	42%	7.5
Moderate	18%	55%	38%	(4 d.f.)
Pioneer	36%	10%	21%	

Note. A traditional occupation is defined as one in which 75% of persons in that field are women, while a pioneer occupation has less than 25% women.

three groups appear to be minimal. Women in the Full-time Group are in more prestigious occupations but this is basically a function of education. There are no differences in intrinsic or extrinsic motivations for work or job satisfaction. Flexibility is, however, greater for women in the Part-time Group.

There are no statistically significant differences on any of these variables for husbands in the three groups (Table 4-4).

Plans Regarding Future Employment

While the general plans regarding employment in the months after childbirth were used to classify women into the three groups, responses to other questions provide further detail.

Both groups of women planning to return to work expect to begin working an average of three months after the baby's birth ($t = .27$, n.s.). However, other details differ between the Full-time and Part-time Groups. Over 90 percent of women in the Full-time Group expect to return to their previous jobs while only 50 percent of the Part-time group do ($\chi^2 = 7.1$, 1 d.f., $p < .01$). Most of the others plan to be self-employed. This is reflected in

Table 4-4.   Decision-Making Variables

Variable	Full-time (N=23) Mean	Part-time (N=21) Mean	Home (N=26) Mean	F	Duncan's Test
Amount of Discussion	1.8	1.8	2.5	4.54*	F,P > H
Amount of Disagreement	4.7	4.7	4.5	.59	
Ease of Decision	2.3	2.4	1.9	1.43	
Definiteness of Decision	1.7	2.6	2.0	3.73*	F > P
Certainty of Plans	1.7	2.5	1.8	3.75**	F,H > P
Comfort With Plans	2.8	2.0	1.6	12.40**	H,P > F
Husband's Comfort With Plans	1.6	1.3	1.6	1.05**	

Note. Except for the last variable, all responses are those reported by the women.
  *$p < .05$.
**$p < .001$.

expected flexibility and the hours during which they plan to work. Women in the Part-time Group are more likely to be working on their own schedules (57 percent as compared to 13 percent, χ^2 = 13.09, 2d.f., $p < .01$) and their jobs will be much more flexible than those working full-time. Seventy-six percent of the Part-time Group will have very flexible or pretty flexible jobs compared to only 30 percent of the Full-time Group (χ^2 = 17.15, 4 d.f., $p < .01$).

Plans for childcare also vary; the majority of women planning to work full-time expect to hire a sitter while the Part-time Group is more likely to have their husbands care for the baby while they are working. Their flexible schedules would make this possible.

A majority of the Home Group (65 percent) expect to work at some point in the future. When asked how old their child would have to be before they considered working, the responses ranged from two years to adulthood, with a mean of 3.7 years. (This number includes only those women who indicated a specific age; 36 percent said they did not know or did not expect to work until their children were grown, if then.)

Women in the Part-time Group were also asked if they would consider working full-time in the future. Thirty-two percent replied "yes," 26 percent "no" and 42 percent said they did not know. Those women (57 percent) who indicated how old their child would have to be before this occurred gave a mean age of 4.3 years.

Decision-Making Process

Couples were asked about the process by which the woman's future employment plans were made, their certainty, and how comfortable they were with the decision. Results show both similarities and differences among groups in these areas (Table 4-4).

The majority of the couples in all groups indicated that employment plans were made jointly by both husband and wife and that there was minimal conflict between spouses regarding this issue. Most of the couples also reported that their decisions were made independently without much influence from parents, friends or colleagues.

While subjects did not speak very much with others about this issue, they do report discussing future plans quite a lot with their spouses. This is particularly true of those in both the Full-time and Part-time Groups. The fact that this issue was discussed to a great extent suggests, first of all, that it is an area in which there is some uncertainty. Couples realize that there is more than one realistic option available and, therefore, a decision needs to be made. If women felt they had no option, there would be little to discuss. The fact that subjects in both working groups report even more discussion between spouses would suggest that the choice was more conflictual for them. One might hypothesize that since working is still not fully sanctioned, choosing this option requires greater consideration.

On the other hand, the women did not report that the decision was particularly difficult, and there were no differences among groups in this regard. The majority, in fact, indicate that it was a very easy or pretty easy decision. This would seem to contradict the fact that so much discussion took place, as well as the literature which indicates that this issue is a difficult one that raises conflicts for many women. Since this sample is comprised only of those women who indicated that they had already made plans, the results of this question are somewhat skewed. Including all women, even those who are undecided, might show a different picture. Further, the literature which deals with women's conflicts focuses on the period after they have children; it is possible that the actual conflict is not clearly felt until then.

Both the Full-time and Home Groups report having made fairly definite arrangements to implement their plans and are relatively certain of carrying them out. There is little indication that they might change their plans after the baby is born. Subjects in the Part-time Group, however, are significantly less definite about their plans and less certain of implementing them. While this, in part, reflects the fact that many are planning to begin new ventures (half are leaving their old jobs) that necessarily involve greater risk and uncertainty, it is also possible that it reflects greater ambivalence on their part.

Having now made their plans, women in the Full-time Group report being significantly less comfortable with their decision than subjects in the other two groups. While many indicate that they would prefer not to work at this time but are doing so because of financial need (as will be discussed later), the discomfort felt by those planning a full-time work involvement when their children are infants is not limited only to this subgroup. Rather, it suggests the continuing anxiety and conflict generally experienced by most women who attempt dual roles; not only are they violating society's norms but their own internalized ones as well.

Interestingly, husbands in both working groups feel significantly more comfortable with their wives' plans than their wives do; this is true for both the Full-time Group ($t = 3.8$, $p < .01$) and the Part-time Group ($t = 2.64$, $p < .05$). It would seem then that this is an issue of particular concern to women. Although husbands appear to play a major role in the decision-making process, they do not seem to experience the conflict as acutely as their wives. This lends support to the hypothesis that the concern women feel about functioning in dual roles reflects not just anxiety about the child's needs being met (since one would expect husbands to be as concerned about the child) but also internalized expectations of themselves as good mothers, and therefore adequate women.

The responses to this set of questions thus elucidate certain distinctions among the three groups. For the Home Group, the decision to continue or interrupt one's career, while not necessarily made without reflection, is not particularly conflictual. These women are relatively definite about their plans and comfortable with their choice.

Women in the Full-time Group are also relatively definite about their plans but much less comfortable with them. For some, it is inconsistent with their own conscious desires; for all, it is a choice that is still relatively in conflict with society's norms. Thus, it is a choice that seems to be, at best, a compromise.

Women in the Part-time Group are considerably less definite about their plans but, like the Home Group, relatively comfortable with them. While their responses suggest that the decision aroused confusion, uncertainty and conflict, they seem to have formulated a resolution which feels satisfactory at this point.

Expressed Motivations

Importance of Factors

Subjects were asked to indicate the importance of various factors to their plans as well as to rank these same factors in order of their saliency. Table 4–5 shows the mean importance of each variable as reported by both women and men in each of the three groups.

The importance of financial reasons was the only variable that significantly differentiates among groups. Both wives and husbands in the Full-time Group rate financial considerations to be more important than couples in either the Part-time or Home Groups.

Needs of the child as well as the wives' own needs were considered to be important factors in all groups, while practical considerations (e.g., availability of childcare) were moderately important. Job opportunities is the least important factor.

Career considerations were of moderate importance in both the Full-time and Part-time Groups while only of slight importance for those in the Home Group. This difference approached significance.

Their husbands' needs were considered to be relatively important in the wives' plans, at least according to the women. The men thought their needs were of less concern in this decision.

Rank Ordering of Factors

When the subjects were forced to choose which factors were of most importance in formulating their plans, their conscious motivations became

Table 4–5. Mean Ratings of Importance of Factors
In Women's Employment Plans

	Groups				
	Full-time (N=23)	Part-time (N=21)	Home (N=26)		Duncan's
Factors	**Mean**	**Mean**	**Mean**	**F**	**Test**
	Women				
Financial Considerations	1.6	2.7	3.1	9.38**	F > P,H
Child's Needs	1.3	1.3	1.0	2.33	
Wife's Needs	1.7	1.3	1.4	1.63	
Husband's Needs	2.3	1.9	1.6	2.07	
Career Considerations	2.6	2.5	3.4	3.01*	F,P > H
Practical Considerations	2.3	2.5	2.4	.09	
Job Opportunities	3.4	3.3	3.9	1.11	
	Men				
Financial Considerations	1.8	3.3	3.6	11.36**	F > P,H
Child's Needs	1.4	1.4	1.0	2.80	
Wife's Needs	1.4	1.3	1.4	0.07	
Husband's Needs	2.8	3.1	3.2	.53	
Career Considerations	2.5	2.7	3.4	2.90	F > H
Practical Considerations	2.4	2.8	2.2	1.45	
Job Opportunities	3.1	3.7	4.0	2.50	

Note. Scales range from 1 (Very Important) to 5 (Not Important).
 * $p < .06$.
 ** $p < .001$.

more clearly delineated. The mean rankings given to each factor by both
wives and husbands are shown in Table 4-6. Also shown, in Table 4-7, is the
distribution of factors cited as the primary reason for the wife's future
employment plans, as well as those ranked second, by wives and husbands in
each group.

These tables show that the mean rankings for the majority of variables
differ among the groups and that each group seems to be motivated by a
different combination of factors.

The mean ranking for financial considerations is significantly different
across groups, with couples in the Full-time Group most often citing this
factor as a major motivation for their plans. In fact, 46 percent of the women
in this group indicate this as their primary reason; another 18 percent rank it
second. In comparison, the Home Group ranks this factor relatively low.
This is logical since those women who plan to interrupt or end their careers
would not cite finances as a reason. Presumably those who did cite financial
considerations mean that the lack of financial need has allowed them to
remain home with their children. Women in the Part-time Group fall

Table 4–6.   Mean Rankings of Motivational Factors

	Groups				
	Full-time (N=23) Mean	Part-time (N=21) Mean	Home (N=26) Mean		
Factors				F	Duncan's Test
		Women			
Financial Considerations	2.8	3.7	4.9	6.32**	F > H
Child's Needs	3.3	2.9	1.1	20.74***	H > P,F
Wife's Needs	2.8	2.0	2.6	2.84*	P > F
Husband's Needs	4.6	4.5	3.7	2.68*	H > F
Career Considerations	3.8	4.8	5.3	4.96*	F > H
Practical Considerations	4.9	4.3	4.3	.95	
Job Opportunities	5.9	5.4	6.1	1.51	
		Men			
Financial Considerations	2.9	4.4	5.1	7.20**	F > P,H
Child's Needs	3.7	3.2	1.2	16.94***	H > P,F
Wife's Needs	2.6	1.6	2.8	5.47**	P > F,H
Husband's Needs	5.1	5.4	5.2	.23	
Career Considerations	3.5	4.3	5.0	5.44**	F > H
Practical Considerations	4.5	3.7	3.0	5.10**	H > F
Job Opportunities	5.6	5.4	5.9	.83	

Note. Ranks range from 1 (most important factor) to 7 (least important factor).
   * $p < .10$.
  ** $p < .01$.
 *** $p < .001$.

between the other two groups. Financial motivations are important, but, in general, not as crucial as other variables. Still, one-third of these women indicate that financial considerations are their first or second most important motivation.

Interestingly, the husbands in the Part-time Group consider financial concerns to be of much less influence in their wives' plans than the wives themselves ($\chi^2 = 5.2$, df = 1, p = .05). Their mean ranking is similar to that of the Home Group and only 11 percent cite this factor as a primary or secondary reason. While husbands in the Full-time Group do agree with their wives that money is an important, motivating force, they too are somewhat less likely than their wives to rank it first or second. Perhaps it is important for these men to feel or at least portray that their wives' employment plans have more to do with other variables besides financial concerns, as this has traditionally been the man's domain; indicating that their wives were going to work to help support the family might be interpreted as a reflection of their own failure. On the other hand, women

Table 4–7. Major Reasons Given For Plans

	Full-time (N=23)		Part-time (N=21)		Home (N=26)	
			Groups			
	Women					
	Primary	Secondary	Primary	Secondary	Primary	Secondary
Financial Considerations	46%	18%	14%	19%	4%	12%
Child's Needs	9%	32%	19%	29%	88%	12%
Wife's Needs	23%	9%	43%	29%	4%	52%
Husband's Needs	0%	14%	0%	10%	0%	12%
Career Considerations	23%	14%	5%	5%	0%	0%
Practical Considerations	0%	5%	14%	10%	4%	12%
Job Opportunities	0%	5%	5%	10%	0%	0%
	Men					
	Primary	Secondary	Primary	Secondary	Primary	Secondary
Financial Considerations	38%	14%	11%	0%	0%	15%
Child's Needs	10%	19%	16%	26%	90%	5%
Wife's Needs	38%	14%	63%	16%	5%	40%
Husband's Needs	0%	10%	0%	0%	0%	0%
Career Considerations	14%	24%	0%	21%	0%	0%
Practical Considerations	0%	14%	5%	37%	5%	40%
Job Opportunities	0%	5%	5%	0%	0%	0%

Note. This table indicates the percentage in each group which rank each factor first (most important) and second.

may be more likely to cite financial motivations since this has always been a relatively acceptable reason for working, even when there are young children.

The needs of the child are, as one might suspect, considered important by all groups, but those in the Home Group rank it significantly higher than couples in the other two groups. In fact, 88 percent of the women planning no employment indicate that their primary reason for doing so is the child; the other 12 percent give this as their second reason. The husbands' rankings are similar. This is consistent with investigators who suggest that the primary reason women stay home is because they feel this is best for the child (Salo, 1977; Wortis, 1971). Only one-third to one-half of subjects in the other two groups indicate that the child's needs are the first or second most significant factor in their decision.

When the relative importance given to the wife's own needs is examined, it is the Part-time Group which ranks this factor highest. Forty-three percent of the women in this group consider their own desires and needs to be the primary motivation for their plans, compared to 23 percent of the women in the Full-time Group and only 4 percent of those in the Home Group. Almost three-quarters of the Part-time Group give their own needs as one of their top two reasons.

Husbands in both working groups tend to rank their wives' needs first or second more often than the women do. The same explanation posited for the differences in husbands' and wives' rankings of financial considerations would operate here as well; that is, it may be more acceptable for husbands to relate their wives' employment to the wives' wishes rather than to financial need while the opposite is true for women.

Career considerations were ranked significantly higher by the Full-time Group than the Home Group, with the Part-time Group being in the middle. Over one-third of women returning to work full-time mentioned this as their first or second reason for doing so; the percentages were negligible for the other groups. Apparently a number of women felt that interrupting their careers would have serious future consequences. Several, in fact, spontaneously wrote that if they stopped working even for a year or two, they would be giving up any chance for promotion and would be losing what they had worked for during the past few years.

Husbands' desires were ranked higher by women in the Home Group compared to those in the Full-time Group, although few cited this as a primary reason. Husbands, in general, ranked their own needs significantly lower than their wives did ($t = 4.18$, $p < .01$).

Practical considerations were ranked relatively low as were job opportunities. Husbands in the Home Group, however, ranked practical factors higher than the Full-time Group. While few ranked this factor first, over 40 percent of husbands in both Home and Part-time Groups said it was a major reason (first or second) for their wives' plans. Significantly fewer wives ($t = 2.51$, $p < .05$) rated it as highly, although it was a major component for some. Written comments concerning this variable indicated that childcare, in particular, was seen as a barrier to working, both in terms of finding quality substitute care and the cost. Many of the women in the Part-time Group, for example, planned to arrange their schedules so that their husbands could take care of the baby while they were working.

Thus, each group is motivated by different sets of factors. The major reason given by women in the Full-time Group for their plans is financial considerations. Almost half cite this as the most important factor, despite the fact that, in this sample, there were no significant differences found in husbands' income. This suggests that either perceived financial need is different across groups or that monetary reasons provide an acceptable justification for working. There is some evidence to support both hypotheses. Although there are no statistical differences in husbands' income, husbands in the Full-time Group tend to earn less than husbands in the other groups. Perhaps more pertinent is the fact that women in the Full-time Group had higher incomes than their counterparts, with this difference approaching significance, and earned a higher percentage of the total family income. Thus it is reasonable to assume that these couples had become used to a standard of living made possible by the addition of the wife's income. Giving up her salary would therefore have the greatest financial impact on this group. Indeed several women commented that although their family incomes seemed high, they had recently bought a new house or had other major expenses which they could not manage with the husband's income alone. In support of the second hypothesis, that financial motivations serve as an appropriate justification for working, is the fact that husbands were less likely to cite monetary motives. In addition, given the income levels of these couples, critical financial need is certainly not apparent. It is also possible that those subjects who cite financial motivations form a subgroup of those planning full-time employment. (This alternative will be explored in greater detail in a later section.)

Two other factors were cited by a substantial number of women in the Full-time Group as their primary reason for future employment; these were the wife's needs and desires, and career considerations. It would seem then that the personal satisfaction received from work was of principal importance to about one-quarter of this group, while career achievement was primary for another quarter. The only other factor that was of import for this group was the child's needs. While few gave this as the major reason, about one-third mentioned this second.

As noted previously, husbands in this group were less likely to cite financial motivations and more likely to mention their wives' desires. Both these factors were given equally as primary and secondary reasons.

For both wives and husbands in the Home Group, the needs of the child clearly took priority in their plans. This was the primary motive mentioned by the vast majority of subjects. For the wives, the major secondary motivation was their own desires and needs, while for their husbands, the wife's needs and practical considerations were of equal secondary importance. The importance of these variables would seem to be a reflection of a strong traditional ideology in this group whereby women are responsible for their children's well-being and good mothering implies staying home with a young child. The fact that over half indicate that this choice reflects their own needs as well may also be viewed as consistent with this ideology; that is, a woman's primary achievement and sense of fulfillment occurs through motherhood. While the majority thus seem happy with this choice, it is noteworthy that their own desires are still secondary.

In many ways, the Part-time Group is most difficult to categorize; a greater variety of major reasons are given by this group than by any other. However, unlike the other groups, the factor that is mentioned most often by both wife and husband is the woman's own desires. Thus these women are generally working out of choice and recognize their plans as such. For the women, important, but secondary, factors are the child's needs and financial considerations while for the men, secondary motivations mentioned include the child, practical elements and, somewhat less often, the wife's career.

Roles

Each subject was asked to rate the importance of three types of roles—work, family and personal—to his or her sense of identity and then to rank these same roles in order of importance. Subjects were also asked to indicate their perceptions of the importance of these same roles to their spouses.

Roles of Women

The majority of roles were rated very important or somewhat important for all groups. The only significant difference among groups was on career or work roles; the importance of these roles for both groups of women planning employment was higher than for the Home Group (a mean of 1.9 compared to 2.7, $F = 4.78$, $p < .01$). The husbands' perceptions were consistent. While women in the Full-time and Part-time Groups thus have a greater investment in their careers and feel it is of greater import to their personal identities than women in the Home Group, this role is still the least important of the three for all groups. More than one-half of the Full-time Group and almost three-quarters of the Part-time Group rank work roles last (Table 4-8). Thus, role priorities for women, at least in this sample, are relatively traditional. For most of the women, home roles clearly take priority over career roles and only in a small percentage is there any indication that they are even equal in importance. In all groups, family roles are ranked highest; that is, subjects feel that these roles are most important to their sense of identity. Personal roles are ranked second by many, especially those women in the Home Group, although there is not a significant difference among groups.

It is interesting to note that the husbands rank their wives' home roles even higher than the women themselves ($t = 2.06$, $p < .05$) and rate personal roles as less important than their wives do ($t = -2.23$, $p < .05$). This is particularly true for the Home Group. One might speculate that they are less willing to have their wives devote energy or give priority to outside activities.

Thus the major difference among the groups of women in this area is that women in both working groups feel that their career roles have greater

Table 4–8. Rankings of Wife's Roles

	Full-time (N=23)	Part-time (N=21)	Home (N=26)
		Groups	
	Wife's Perception		
Work Roles			
First	13%	0%	4%
Second	30%	29%	4%
Third	57%	71%	92%
Family Roles			
First	52%	67%	62%
Second	39%	29%	31%
Third	9%	5%	4%
Personal Roles			
First	35%	33%	35%
Second	30%	43%	62%
Third	35%	24%	4%
	Husband's Perception		
Work Roles			
First	14%	5%	0%
Second	41%	21%	13%
Third	46%	74%	87%
Family Roles			
First	68%	79%	87%
Second	14%	21%	13%
Third	14%	0%	0%
Personal Roles			
First	9%	16%	13%
Second	50%	58%	74%
Third	36%	26%	13%

personal significance than do women in the Home Group. Significantly, those women planning to continue their careers have not replaced the traditional roles of wife and mother but have expanded their roles in life, and broadened their self-identities, to include that of worker.

Roles of Men

There were no significant differences among groups in the importance of roles to the men in this sample, as rated by either the men themselves or their wives. All roles were very or somewhat important to the majority in all groups, with personal roles somewhat, though not significantly, less prominent.

When we examine the distribution of rankings, however, differences among groups do emerge. The husbands' self-rankings (Table 4-9) indicate that husbands in both the Full-time and Part-time Groups rank family roles as more important to their self-identities than men in the Home Group. Almost twice as many men in the former groups rank it first compared to those in the latter group. Thus, for men in the Full-time and Part-time Groups, family roles are considered most salient to their personal identities. For the Home Group, about the same number give priority to career roles as to family roles.

The wives' perceptions of their husbands' roles reveal similar results (Table 4-9). Women in the Full-time and Part-time Groups tend to perceive their husbands' home roles as being more important and their career roles less important to their husbands' self-identities compared to the perceptions of women in the Home group.

Thus, in general, men in the Home Group are more likely to perceive their careers as their most salient role, while men in the Full-time and Part-time Groups perceive greater saliency in their home roles. The husband's maintaining of a balance between work and family would seem to be critical in allowing a woman to successfully pursue her own career interests. It would be difficult to maintain a career commitment if one's husband considered his work to be most important while family matters were secondary, unless there were no children involved. For those in both working groups, then, the wife's expanded roles seem to be, at least in part, compensated for by the husband's expansion of his own roles.

Role Combinations

Table 4-10 shows the distribution of couples' role priorities. Those subjects who ranked family roles higher than career roles were said to give priority to family roles; those who ranked career roles higher were said to give priority to their work. The combination of priorities for each couple was compared across groups. The pattern in which the wife gives priority to family roles while her husband gives priority to career roles is significantly more likely to occur in the Home Group.

Thus, the role pattern for couples in the Home Group are relatively traditional; it seems that the woman sees her primary source of fulfillment in

Table 4-9. Rankings of Husband's Roles

	Groups		
	Full-time *(N=23)*	*Part-time* *(N=21)*	*Home* *(N=26)*
	Husband's Perception		
Work Roles			
First	18%	16%	44%
Second	46%	32%	35%
Third	32%	47%	22%
Family Roles			
First	64%	68%	35%
Second	27%	21%	52%
Third	9%	11%	13%
Personal Roles			
First	5%	16%	13%
Second	41%	42%	30%
Third	55%	37%	57%
	Wife's Perception		
Work Roles			
First	35%	24%	54%
Second	22%	62%	19%
Third	44%	14%	19%
Family Roles			
First	44%	62%	27%
Second	39%	19%	54%
Third	13%	19%	12%
Personal Roles			
First	17%	14%	15%
Second	15%	19%	23%
Third	44%	67%	62%

the home while her husband's is most often at work. The pattern is different for those in the other groups. While the wife still gives priority to family roles, career roles are now more salient, and for her husband, greater priority is now given to the family roles. Although role reversal has by no means

Table 4–10.   Distribution of Couples' Role Priorities

		Groups			
		Full-time (N=23)	Part-time (N=21)	Home (N=26)	χ^2
Role Priority					
Wife	*Husband*				
Home	Home	74%	74%	40%	9.35*
Home	Career	10%	20%	55%	(2 d.f.)[a]
Career	Career	5%	5%	5%	
Career	Home	10%	0%	0%	

[a] The last two rows were not included in the statistical analysis.

* $p < .01$.

occurred, each has moved towards the other so that there is greater role-sharing.

Husband's Support

Two specific questions were asked of all subjects to assess the husband's support of his wife's career: how positively or negatively the husband feels about his wife having a career, and how supportive he has been of her career endeavors (Tables 4-11 and 4-12).

There was a significant difference among groups on the wives' perceptions of both their husbands' attitudes and their support. Women in both the Full-time and Part-time Groups indicated that their husbands had more positive attitudes than the Home Group. Over three-quarters of the women in the two working groups felt their husbands were very positive compared to one-half of the Home Group; one-third of the latter felt their husbands were only neutral or somewhat negative. Similarly, women in the working groups felt their husbands were significantly more supportive of their careers.

Thus, those women who plan to continue employment perceive a positive, supportive attitude on the part of their husbands. This is consistent with studies which indicate that support by one's husband or boyfriend is crucial if a woman is to continue her career (Epstein, 1970; Rapoport and Rapoport, 1976) and suggests that women may base their plans at least partially on their perception of their husband's attitudes.

When the husbands' responses are examined, it is apparent that the women's perceptions are relatively consistent with the husbands' reported attitudes. Again, men in both the Full-time and Part-time Groups report

Table 4–11. Husband's Attitude Toward Wife's Career

	Groups			
	Full-time (N=23)	*Part-time (N=21)*	*Home (N=26)*	χ^2
		Wife's Perception		
Very Positive	87%	76%	50%	8.49*
Somewhat Positive	13%	19%	15%	(2 d.f.)[a]
Neutral	0%	5%	31%	
Somewhat Negative	0%	0%	4%	
		Husband's Perception		
Very Positive	86%	68%	44%	9.26**
Somewhat Positive	9%	21%	30%	(2 d.f.)[a]
Neutral	5%	11%	17%	
Somewhat Negative	0%	0%	9%	

[a] The "Somewhat Positive", "Neutral", and "Somewhat Negative" categories were combined in the statistical analysis.
* $p < .05$.
** $p < .01$.

significantly more positive attitudes toward their wives' careers than husbands in the Home Group. Thus the wives' perceptions are not just an attempt to validate their plans but are based on a realistic appraisal of the husbands' true (or at least conscious) feelings. Although the men's responses regarding support of their wives' careers do not differ significantly across groups, the trend is similar to that observed by the women.

Table 4–12. Husband's Support of Wife's Career

	Groups			
	Full-time (N=23)	*Part-time (N=21)*	*Home (N=26)*	χ^2
		Wife's Responses		
Active and Unconditional	91%	71%	58%	7.0*
Unconditional But Inactive	4%	29%	28%	(2.d.f.)[a]
Conditional	4%	0%	19%	
		Husband's Responses		
Active and Unconditional	68%	63%	52%	1.27
Unconditional But Inactive	18%	32%	26%	(2 d.f.)[b]
Conditional	14%	5%	17%	
Resigned	0%	0%	4%	

[a] The last two categories were combined in the statistical analysis.
[b] The last two categories were combined in the statistical analysis.
* $p < .05$.

Personality Variables

Responses on the PRF were converted to *t*-scores according to the norms given in the Manual (Jackson, 1974). As indicated by Table 4-13, there were no significant differences found among the three groups on any of the personality variables in question, either for the women or their husbands.

These results are somewhat surprising, given past research and theories regarding the relationship between personality variables and women's employment. Perhaps these groups differ not in regard to general personality traits but rather in regard to the context in which they express these traits. For example, a high achievement score reflects an individual who is purposeful, industrious and capable. It is possible that while women in all three groups scored similarly on this variable, the groups differ in the means through which they fulfill these needs; the Full-time Group may achieve at work while the Home Group achieve by being extremely competent homemakers and mothers or feel a sense of achievement through assisting in their husbands' accomplishments.

However, the fact remains that the groups were similar on these variables; women who plan to interrupt their careers do not indicate different personality needs from those who plan to continue working full- or part-time. This would suggest that plans regarding home and career roles, at least at this stage, are not based on individual personality needs but rather on other, perhaps more external, factors.

Sex Role Attitudes

Sex-Role Attitude Scales

Despite the fact that subjects in general endorsed relative nontyping of roles by gender, there were substantial differences among the groups in regard to sex-role attitudes (Table 4-14). Those in the Full-time Group express significantly more egalitarian attitudes toward male and female roles while couples in the Home Group reveal more traditional, sex-typed views. The means of subjects in the Part-time Group are between those of the other two groups. Statistically, however, the women in the Part-time Group have scores that are more similar to women in the Home Group while their husbands' scores are closer to husbands in the Full-time Group.

To better understand the meaning of these differences, scores on the various subscales need to be examined. Only two of the revised subscales reveal group differences for both the women and their husbands: the Familial Role scale and the Dual Roles scale. The first measures attitudes toward men's and women's roles in the family, while the latter reflects attitudes toward the ability of professional women to meet their family

Table 4–13. Personality Scores

	Full-time (N=23) Mean	Part-time (N=21) Mean	Home (N=26) Mean	F	Duncan's Test
		Women			
Achievement	51.3	50.8	49.9	.21	
Affiliation	47.7	45.6	48.1	.37	
Autonomy	45.4	47.4	47.1	.30	
Change	41.4	42.9	45.9	1.86	
Dominance	53.5	50.3	50.0	1.13	
Nurturance	46.4	46.1	49.2	.88	
Social Recognition	46.5	47.1	47.6	.09	
Succorance	43.7	47.0	45.0	.63	
		Men			
Achievement	52.2	55.2	51.1	1.46	
Affiliation	49.7	49.7	50.9	.09	
Autonomy	44.7	39.8	44.8	2.17	
Change	47.0	41.7	46.8	1.63	
Dominance	52.2	52.3	50.7	.24	
Nurturance	52.6	51.1	51.0	.26	
Social Recognition	49.9	46.6	47.9	.46	
Succorance	47.0	50.2	47.6	.76	

responsibilities when they have full-time jobs. Subjects in the Full-time Group hold more modern views about roles in the family compared to the Home Group. The latter are more likely to endorse traditional assumptions, such as, that it is important for mothers to remain home with their children, particularly when they are young, and that the home is a woman's primary responsibility. The Full-time Group, on the other hand, are more likely to indicate that women should work if they choose and that men should be involved to a greater extent in the home. The mean score of women in the Part-time Group is not significantly different from either of the other groups, although their husbands' scores are again similar to those of husbands in the Full-time Group.

The differences on the Dual Roles scale are consistent with this and provide further insight. Not only do subjects in the Home Group feel that a mother's place is at home with her young child, but also that a woman who works full-time cannot be as good a wife and mother. In contrast, couples in the Full-time group are more likely to express the view that a woman can successfully fulfill the demands of both a family and a career. To what extent

Table 4–14. Mean Scores On Sex-Role Attitude Scales

| | Groups | | | | |
	Full-time (N=23) Mean	Part-time (N=21) Mean	Home (N=26) Mean	*F*	Duncan's Test
		Women			
Total SRA Score	73.5	81.8	87.4	6.35**	H,P > F
Revised Osmond-Martin Scale	44.0	49.6	52.3	3.80*	H > F
Familial Roles	12.7	15.4	18.2	7.70***	H > F
Extrafamilial Roles	6.1	5.8	6.5	.43	
Stereotypes	14.1	15.6	15.3	.93	
Need For Social Change	11.1	12.8	12.4	1.10	
Dual Roles Scale	6.8	9.8	11.9	11.28***	H,P > F
Value of Motherhood	22.6	22.5	23.2	.19	
		Men			
Total SRA Score	86.8	94.5	102.1	3.43*	H > F
Revised Osmond-Martin Scale	55.0	60.9	65.2	1.96	
Familial Roles	15.3	16.6	20.1	5.31**	H > P,F
Extrafamilial Roles	8.9	9.3	8.8	.07	
Stereotypes	19.0	18.3	19.9	.26	
Need For Social Change	11.9	15.7	15.8	4.36*	H,P > F
Dual Roles Scale	9.3	10.1	14.1	9.18***	H > P,F
Value of Motherhood	22.4	23.5	23.1	.28	

Note. Higher scores reflect more Traditional attitudes.
* $p < .05$.
** $p < .01$.
*** $p < .001$.

these differences accurately reflect preexisting attitudes is not known. It is possible that each group is merely justifying its future plans. For instance, it would be difficult for a woman who is planning to work to believe that this will be harmful to her marriage or to her child's well-being. Likewise, women planning no career involvement may feel, with today's feminist ideology being publicized, that they need to justify their lack of employment.

Women in the Part-time Group express attitudes more similar, statistically, to women in the Home Group, suggesting some ambivalence on their part. While they do not necessarily believe that a woman should be a full-time homemaker, they express concern that working full-time would impede the fulfillment of responsibilities a woman has to her family. It is interesting to note that their husbands' views are again more similar to husbands in the Full-time Group than to those in the Home Group, reflecting support of their wives' dual roles. All groups express favorable attitudes toward mothers and do not at all feel that others demean this role. Thus, the differences among groups do not reflect varying beliefs about the value of motherhood per se, but rather the need for exclusive mothering by women.

The other subscales do not indicate any differences among the women in the three groups, suggesting that variant attitudes toward sex roles are specific to the context of the family. This is consistent with research indicating that equal rights and non-sex-typing in the labor market and other areas are endorsed more frequently than equal rights in the home (Araji, 1977; Mason, et al., 1976). In other words, while there may be abstract support for egalitarianism, more conservative attitudes prevail when the individual's own behavior and personal life are involved; behavior change often lags behind attitudinal change.

Men in the Full-time Group, in addition, express more liberal views concerning social change than do men in the Part-time or Home Groups. This subscale measures the extent to which one believes that social action (legislation for equal rights, better day care facilities, equal employment opportunities, etc.) should be taken to ensure equality between the sexes. It would appear then that husbands in the Full-time Group have a greater commitment to such equality. They are not merely paying lip-service to abstract ideals which are considered fashionable today, but they express a greater willingness to actively support these ideals as well as make changes in their own lives that are more consistent with expressed beliefs.

Thus, in general, both women and men in the Full-time Group are more likely to express attitudes toward male and female roles which reflect less sex differentiation than subjects in the Home Group. This is most pronounced in regard to familial roles. Those in the Part-time Group express views that are more moderate in comparison; however, the women generally respond more similarly to women in the Home Group while their husbands' attitudes show greater similarity with the men in the Full-time Group.

Norms

Specific items in the questionnaire asked subjects about their normative expectations in regard to financial responsibility, household tasks and childcare, as well as expectations of their actual behavior.

Couples in the Full-time Group were significantly more likely to indicate that spouses should be equally responsible for both financial provision of the family and taking care of household tasks, compared to couples in either the Part-time or Home Groups (Tables 4-15 and 4-16). Reported behavior regarding household tasks was relatively consistent with expressed norms; a greater number of spouses in the Full-time Group shared these responsibilities (65 percent, according to the women) than couples in the Part-time or Home Groups (38 percent and 31 percent, respectively). Interestingly, subjects tended to indicate a greater willingness to share responsibility for their spouse's traditional role than the spouse was to have them share it. For example, the women expressed more egalitarian norms regarding financial support than the men did ($t = 2.5, p < .05$). Likewise, the men tended to endorse equal responsibility for household tasks more than their wives, although this difference was not significant. One might hypothesize that subjects hold deeply rooted traditional expectations of themselves, regardless of their consciously expressed views. Not meeting these expectations would be experienced as personal failure while adding additional responsibilities would not reflect on them negatively.

This is even more apparent in regard to childcare (Table 4-17). Men in both working groups tend to endorse equal responsibility in this area more than their wives do, although not significantly so. Further, women in both working groups were less likely to think that childcare should be equally shared as compared to other traditionally sex-typed responsibilities while the reverse was true for women in the Home Group. Even less expected that this responsibility would actually be shared equally, although in some cases the husband was expected to be involved in childcare more than the wife (Table 4-18).

Table 4-15. Norm for Financial Provision of Family

	Full-time (N=23)	Part-time (N=21)	Home (N=26)	χ^2
		Groups		
	Women's Responses			
Equal	73%	38%	31%	7.85*
Husband More Than Wife	23%	43%	58%	(2 d.f.)[a]
Mainly Husband	5%	19%	12%	
	Men's Responses			
Equal	59%	21%	17%	11.85
Husband More Than Wife	32%	47%	44%	(4 d.f.)
Mainly Husband	9%	32%	39%	

[a] The "Husband More" and "Mainly Husband" categories were combined in the statistical analysis.

* $p < .05$.

Table 4–16. Norm for Household Tasks

| | Groups | | | |
	Full-time (N=23)	Part-time (N=21)	Home (N=26)	χ^2
	Women's Responses			
Equal	74%	43%	43%	6.18*
Wife More Than Husband	26%	43%	50%	(2 d.f.)[a]
Mainly Wife	0%	14%	8%	
	Men's Responses			
Equal	82%	53%	48%	6.32*
Wife More Than Husband	14%	42%	44%	(2 d.f.)[a]
Mainly Wife	5%	5%	9%	

[a] The "Wife More Than Husband" and "Mainly Wife" categories were combined in the statistical analysis.
* $p < .05$.

These responses again seem to reflect deeply seated norms that are difficult to surrender in one's own life, although they may be less valued in the abstract. The mother's responsibility for childcare is a fundamental assumption in the traditional ideology, one that has been shown to be widely accepted. It would seem then that women are generally unwilling to give up this role. One might hypothesize that, at least in part, it is a reflection of guilt; those women who are actually planning exclusive mothering appear more willing to share these responsibilities while those planning to work experience greater conflict and therefore may attempt to overcompensate for their perceived neglect. In part, it is also a reflection of an unrealistic

Table 4–17. Norm for Childcare

| | Groups | | | |
	Full-time (N=23)	Part-time (N=21)	Home (N=26)	χ^2
	Women's Responses			
Equal	57%	30%	58%	4.22
Wife More Than Husband	30%	70%	35%	(2 d.f.)[a]
Mainly Wife	13%	0%	8%	
	Men's Responses			
Equal	73%	42%	44%	5.18
Wife More Than Husband	18%	37%	48%	(2 d.f.)[a]
Mainly Wife	9%	21%	9%	

[a] The "Wife More Than Husband" and "Mainly Wife" categories were combined in the statistical analysis.

Table 4–18.   Expectations for Childcare

	Groups			
	Full-time *(N=23)*	*Part-time* *(N=21)*	*Home* *(N=26)*	χ^2
	Women's Perceptions			
Mainly Wife	9%	19%	23%	3.49
Wife More Than Husband	57%	67%	46%	(2 d.f.)[a]
Equally	22%	10%	31%	
Husband More Than Wife	13%	0%	0%	
Mainly Husband	0%	5%	0%	
	Men's Perceptions			
Mainly Wife	5%	11%	4%	10.68*
Wife More Than Husband	32%	74%	65%	(2 d.f.)[a]
Equally	59%	16%	30%	
Husband More Than Wife	5%	0%	0%	

[a] The "Mainly Wife" and "Wife More Than Husband" categories and the "Equally", "Husband More Than Wife" and "Mainly Husband" categories were combined in the statistical analysis.

* $p < .01$.

commitment to the "superwoman" role. Despite the responsibilities of a job, these women expect to take major responsibility for childcare as well. This is consistent with studies of dual-career families in which the women were often preoccupied with being able to maintain their traditional housewife roles and were reluctant to have husbands share family responsibilities (Johnson and Johnson, 1977; Poloma and Garland, 1971). This seems to be especially true in regard to childcare because it is such an essential part of a woman's self-identity.

It is notable that women in the Part-time Group, in particular, did not expect childcare to be shared equally, despite the fact that in 40 percent of the cases, the husband would be taking care of the baby while his wife was working. Perhaps the women in this group feel an even greater responsibility to meet their traditional obligations because it was their choice to maintain a career involvement. If they felt they had to work for monetary reasons (as so many of the Full-time women do), they would feel more comfortable receiving "help" from their husbands.

Subjects were also asked to indicate the minimum age a child should be before the mother returns to work by choice. Not surprisingly, couples in the Full-time and Part-time Groups felt the mother could be employed significantly earlier than those in the Home Group ($\chi^2 = 26.73$, 4 d.f., $p < .001$ for the women). Sixty-five percent of the Full-time Group and 67 percent of the Part-time Group felt that a mother could return to work when a child was less than one year old compared to only 8 percent of the Home Group. Husbands' responses were similar. There were no differences in how subjects felt their mothers or society in general would respond to the same question. However, women in the working groups tended to feel that a mother should be able to return to work earlier than they thought society, in general, would approve of ($t = 5.18$, $p < .01$ for the Full-time Group; $t = 4.14$, $p < .01$ for the Part-time Group). Their greater discomfort with their plans would seem to be a reflection of this.

In summary, differences among groups regarding sex-role attitudes were revealed, with the Full-time Group being more likely to express modern attitudes while the Home Group held more traditional views; differences emerged particularly in regard to the family sphere.

In addition, responses indicated that for all groups, egalitarian, non-differentiated sex roles were endorsed to a greater extent in the abstract, with subjects being less willing to incorporate these ideals into their own lives.

Revised Groups

Subjects were asked what their ideal plan would be if financial considerations, husband's desires and child's needs were not factors. The results indicate that 76 percent of the women in the Part-time Group and 80 percent of those in the Home Group have made plans that are syntonic with their ideal choices. Only 35 percent of the women in the Full-time Group, however, indicate that they would ideally choose to work full-time, while 30 percent would prefer part-time employment and another 30 percent would choose to remain home.

It seemed likely then that the Full-time Group, more than the other groups, was composed of subgroups whose characteristics and attitudes might be very different from each other. The fact that almost half of the Full-time Group cited financial considerations as their primary reason for working provided support for this hypothesis. Hoffman's (1975) warning that other considerations, like motivation for work, must be taken into account when comparing groups thus appeared quite relevant.

To further explore the hypothesis that the Full-time Group was composed of two or more subgroups, women in the Full-time Group (and their husbands) were categorized into three separate groups depending on the wife's ideal preference. Because of the small number in each group, nonparametric statistics were used to analyze potential variations.

Not surprisingly, the greatest difference among these subgroups related to their stated motivations (Table 4-19). Financial motivations were significantly more salient for both the women who preferred to remain home and those who preferred part-time employment, while women who wanted to continue full-time career involvement listed their own desires and needs as

Table 4–19.   Motivational Factors of Subgroups Within Full-time Group

| | Ideal Preference | | | |
	Full-time (N=8)		Part-time (N=7)		Home (N=7)		χ^2
	Mean Importance of Reasons						
Financial							
Considerations	2.3		1.4		1.0		8.60*
Child's Needs	1.0		1.1		2.0		8.30*
Practical							
Considerations	1.9		2.6		2.7		1.90
Wife's Needs	1.1		1.7		2.5		5.70
Career							
Considerations	2.3		2.6		3.3		1.10
Husband's Needs	2.4		1.7		3.0		4.10
Job Opportunities	3.3		3.9		3.2		.83

	Major Reasons Given					
	Primary	**Secondary**	**Primary**	**Secondary**	**Primary**	**Secondary**
Financial						
Considerations	13%	25%	57%	14%	83%	17%
Child's Needs	0%	25%	29%	29%	0%	33%
Practical						
Considerations	0%	0%	0%	14%	0%	0%
Wife's Needs	63%	0%	0%	14%	0%	17%
Career						
Considerations	25%	25%	14%	0%	17%	17%
Husband's Needs	0%	25%	0%	14%	0%	0%
Job Opportunities	0%	0%	0%	0%	0%	17%

Note. As reported by the women.
* $p < .05$.

their primary motivation. Career considerations were also considered quite important to the latter group: 50 percent indicated this to be a major motivation. Likewise, this group tended to attach more importance to their work roles, particularly in comparison to the Home-Preferred subgroup.

Otherwise, there were few statistically significant differences among these subgroups. (When differences did emerge, women who preferred part-time employment were generally more similar to the Full-time Preferred subgroup than to the Home Preferred subgroup.) Those preferring to remain home were older and had more job experience but were no different in achieved educational level, income or occupational characteristics. They were, as expected, less comfortable with their plans but no less definite about their decision. Interestingly, 57 percent of the women in the Home-Preferred Group indicated that the pregnancy was not planned compared to none of the Full-time Preferred subgroup and only 14 percent of the Part-time Preferred subgroup. This would suggest some ambivalence on their part and indicate that, as a group, they were less ready to begin a family. Whether this was due to financial concerns, conflictual feelings about parenthood or other factors is not known.

Sex-role attitudes were similar except that women in the work-preferred subgroups were more likely to believe a woman could successfully manage dual roles and that she should work if she chooses to, regardless of the age of her child. Personality variables of wives and husbands were also similar across groups. However, there was a difference in autonomy that approached significance, with those women who preferred to remain home manifesting the greatest need for autonomy ($\chi^2 = 5.83$, $p < .06$). Since it might be expected that a higher need for autonomy would characterize those women who preferred to return to work, this anomolous result raises the hypothesis that the women in the Home Preferred Subgroup may be motivated to return to work partly by an unconscious need to maintain a sense of independence.

This data lends further support to the suggestion made earlier that the financial motivations cited by these subjects are, at least in part, a socially acceptable justification for working. The Home-Preferred Subgroup, while maintaining that financial considerations were their main reason for future employment, had incomes that were no lower than those returning to work for more personal reasons. The fact that these women were slightly older and had been in the labor force for a longer period of time suggests that their consumption patterns may have become adapted to a relatively high level of income which was difficult to abandon. In addition, even a few years' age difference in these changing times may make it more difficult for this cohort to feel justified in working by choice when they have young children; fewer of their peers would be likely to have supportive attitudes.

While the small size of these subgroups makes it difficult to validly analyze group differences, there are some indications that the Home-Preferred Subgroup may indeed form a separate subgroup, including their different conscious motivations for employment, a greater need for autonomy and the lack of a consistent pattern in their responses.

In a further effort to determine whether those women who planned employment against their conscious wishes comprised a distinct group, four subgroups were formed and data again analyzed. The four subgroups were as follows:

Full-time Syntonic. Comprised of fifteen women who planned full-time employment and expressed a preference for some work involvement; i.e., the Full-time and Part-time Preferred Subgroups of the original Full-time

Group. These two subsets were combined because the previous analysis indicated that they were quite similar.

Work Dystonic. Comprised of the seven women in the Home-Preferred Subgroup as well as two women in the Part-time Group who indicated they would prefer to remain home. Thus these women were planning employment but ideally would have chosen not to work at all.

Part-time Syntonic. Comprised of the eighteen women who were planning part-time employment and had chosen this option as their ideal choice.

Home Syntonic. Comprised of the twenty women who were planning to remain home and indicated that this was their ideal preference.

In addition to further exploring the characteristics of the Work Dystonic Group, it was thought that isolating this group might allow further differences to emerge among the other groups that may have been masked previously.

This analysis, however, added only minimally to our understanding of group differences. In general, the same variables that differentiated the original groups were again salient, although in some instances the relationships were intensified. For example, the Full-time and Part-time Syntonic Groups' scores on the Sex-Role Attitude Scales tended to be weighted even more toward the modern, nondifferentiated end of the continuum, while the Work Dystonic Group was closer to the Home Syntonic Group.

Only a few novel differences actually emerged among the revised groups. Husband's income in the Full-time Syntonic and Work Dystonic groups was significantly lower compared to the Part-time Syntonic Group ($F = 3.6$, $p < .05$), but not the Home Syntonic Group. Thus, there is some evidence that financial motivations are realistic; however, there still remains no difference in income level between women working primarily for monetary reasons and women working full-time primarily for other, more personal, reasons.

Differences among the groups also arose on subjects' perceptions of how their mothers would respond to the question regarding the minimum age a child should be before his/her mother works by choice. Women in both Syntonic working groups felt their mothers had more "liberal" attitudes in this area; i.e., they were more likely to approve of a mother working earlier ($\chi^2 = 7.95$, df = 3, $p < .05$). Husbands in the Full-time Syntonic Group were also more likely to perceive a liberal attitude on their mothers' parts than husbands in any of the other three groups ($\chi^2 = 12.41$, df = 3, $p < .01$). While no other questions related to subjects' family backgrounds were asked, responses to this question suggest that those women planning to work "by choice" had mothers who encouraged career involvement and did not believe as strongly in the traditional ideology. Likewise, husbands of those women planning to work full-time by choice had mothers who are more supportive of dual roles for women, an attitude which no doubt their sons identified with. This is consistent with studies of the relationship between maternal employment and attitudes and daughter's career salience as well as children's sex-role attitudes (Baruch, 1972; Vogel, et al., 1970).

In summary, the small number of subjects in the Work Dystonic Group and the generally inconsistent, confusing results make it difficult to accurately characterize this group. While removing them from the original groups makes these more homogeneous (within each particular group), it is not at all clear that the Work Dystonic subjects form a distinct subgroup of their own. Certainly it is not valid to conclude that they all closely resemble the Home Group except for the fact that they have less income. Nor can one assume that they have unconscious motivations for working but find financial reasons to be more acceptable both to themselves and others.

There is some indication that there is more than one pattern that characterizes members of this group. In particular, on many of the variables (e.g., marital satisfaction, importance of career role, ranking of own needs, etc.), subjects in this group were at both extremes. Perhaps both potential hypotheses offerred above are valid for particular members of this subgroup. That is, for some, the desire to remain home with their child is quite strong but economic factors make this impossible. For others, a desire to maintain a high standard of living in combination with other benefits of working (e.g., greater independence) are enough to outweigh their conscious norms regarding the role of women, despite the fact that this remains uncomfortable and conflictual.

Discriminant Analyses

The preceding analyses show that there are a number of individual variables on which the three groups significantly differ. To further our understanding of these differences, and to begin to identify those variables, or sets of variables, that contribute most to the differentiation among groups of subjects, discriminant analysis was utilized. The discriminant analysis program from the Statistical Package for the Social Sciences (SPSS) was used for this analysis (Klecka, 1975).

Discriminant analysis is a multivariate technique in which variables are weighted and linearly combined into one or more functions to achieve the maximum possible statistical separation among groups. The stepwise method that was used in the present investigation proceeds by choosing among a set of variables the one that will best discriminate among the groups. It then selects the variable which, when combined with the first, will most contribute to further differentiation. This is continued until additional variables will no longer improve the power of the discriminant function.

This type of analysis can be used to investigate several questions. First, by examining which variables in a given set are included in the function(s), we can determine which ones differentiate the groups, when other overlapping variables are partialled out. Second, by inspecting the weights (i.e., standardized coefficients) assigned, the relative contribution of each variable may be ascertained. Third, it is possible to analyze how well particular functions do differentiate among the groups by calculating a multivariate analog to the "estimated w^2" (Tatsuoka, 1970). A more intuitive approach to this last question can be followed by determining the percentage of cases which, using the discriminant function, would be correctly classified, although this is not totally correlated with the estimated w^2.

The present analysis sought to explore these questions by first analyzing different sets of variables separately (demographic and occupational characteristics, decision-making variables, personality variables, motivational factors, importance of roles and attitudinal variables), then combining discriminating variables into a final set of functions. Variables that related to the particular factor (and were measured by means of an ordinal or interval scale) were entered into the separate analyses. These results are reported in greater detail elsewhere (Behrman, 1980). Those variables which proved to have significant differentiating power were then included in the final array of variables. A word of caution is indicated at this point. Because (a) the discriminant analyses were not based on specifically formulated hypotheses, (b) the sample size was small, and (c) the question of multicorrelinearity was not addressed, these analyses must be considered purely exploratory.

Table 4-20 summarizes the analysis using the total array of variables. Several analytic attempts yielded basically the same group of variables, indicating their particular relevancy to this issue. Two significant functions emerged, with 81 percent of the variance accounted for. Using these variables, 90 percent of the cases were correctly classified. Clearly then, it is possible to differentiate the three groups on a variety of variables; that is, we can conclude that women who plan to stay home with their child are different in some ways from those who expect to return to work full-time. In addition, it can be seen that women in the Part-time Group are distinct from the other two groups, indicating that including them in one of the other groups may be based on erroneous assumptions.

Examining those variables which best differentiated the groups, it can be seen that several types of variables are represented. The majority, though, appear to reflect attitudinal variables; that is, how subjects view their current roles, both abstractly and in their personal lives. For the women, the differences among groups seem to relate particularly to their assumptions regarding needs of the child. Women in the Home Group are more likely to

Table 4-20.   Discriminant Analysis with Total Array of Variables

Variables as Entered Stepwise in the Function[a]		Significance of Increment in Rao's V	Standardized Discriminant Coefficients	
			Function 1	Function 2
1. Rank—Child's Needs (Women)		.000	.6626	−.7534
2. Comfortableness with Plans (Women)		.000	.7429	.4026
3. Dual Roles Scale (Women)		.000	−.4311	−.3305
4. Definiteness of Plans (Women)		.000	−.2209	−.7609
5. Importance of Wife's Work Role (Women)		.000	−.2780	.4453
6. Importance of Financial Considerations (Women)		.001	−.2534	−.3586
7. Autonomy (Women)		.018	−.3252	−.1459
8. Wife's Education (Removed at step 12)		.009		
9. Extrafamilial Roles (Men)		.011	.6848	−.2673
10. Rank—Husband's Family Roles (Men)		.000	−.3377	.3250
11. Need for Social Change (Men)		.002	−.4553	−.2414

F'n	Eigenvalue	Relative Per Cent	Canonical Correlation	After Function	Wilks Lambda	Chi-Square	d.f.	Sign.
1	2.433	80.63	.84	0	.184	105.846	20	.000
2	.584	19.37	.61	1	.631	28.764	9	.001

CLASSIFICATION PREDICTION OUTCOMES

		Predicted Group Membership			Centroids	
Actual Group	n	1	2	3	Function 1	Function 2
Full-time (1)	23	22 (96.0%)	1 (4.0%)	0 (0%)	1.9020	.5235
Part-time (2)	21	2 (10.0%)	18 (86.0%)	1 (5.0%)	.0837	−1.1418
Home (3)	26	1 (4.0%)	2 (8.0%)	23 (86.0%)	−1.7501	.4595

Percent of Cases Correctly Classified: 90%
[a] The parenthetical indicates which subjects the variable refers to.

believe that a young child needs a full-time mother and their plans are based primarily on this assumption. Having a career at this time would therefore be incompatible with being a "good" mother, a role that is extremely important to them. Women in the Full-time Group, on the other hand, do not believe that being a good mother necessitates giving up one's career; therefore, they have maintained their career interests.

The attitudes of the husbands in each group are also salient. Those variables which contribute to the differentiation across groups are the husbands' attitudes toward male and female roles outside the family, their perception of the need for social change and the relative importance of family roles to their sense of identity. (It is probable that their views of family roles were consistent with their wives' and therefore did not contribute additional information, while the wives' views of abstract social roles were generally fairly liberal across all groups.) These first two variables would seem to represent the husband's commitment to sexual equality and nondifferentiation, and thus may be the most accurate indicator of his values in this area. The importance of their family roles would seem to be a reflection of this commitment in their own lives.

The only personality variable which contributed to the discriminant function was autonomy, again suggesting that the plans women make to continue or interrupt their careers at this time are based on factors other than personality needs.

The importance of financial considerations also made a moderate contribution in this analysis, representing the economic realities that confront many families today. Notice, however, that other variables besides financial considerations were much more salient in discriminating among groups. In other words, while financial motives may be important, they do not completely explain why women choose to continue or interrupt their careers. The other two variables which appear are definiteness of and comfort with plans, both reflecting conflictual feelings about this issue.

Thus the differences among the groups, while multidimensional, seem to represent primarily alternative views regarding current sex-roles and beliefs regarding the needs of a child.

5

Discussion of Overall Findings

While the previous chapter described group variations on the individual factors investigated in some detail, this section will emphasize the salient, overall patterns that emerged, as well as discuss some of the more relevant and interesting implications.

The purpose of this study was to further our understanding of the factors that are related to a woman's decision to continue or interrupt her career at the birth of her first child. Demographic and occupational characteristics of women and their husbands, personality traits and sex-role attitudes were among the variables investigated. Although many of these same variables had been investigated individually in previous research, this study sought to explore a variety of seemingly relevant variables at one point in time.

Other major differences between past research and the current study related to the time at which subjects were studied and the population chosen. Previous research, in general, had focused on differences between groups of college women or between working women and homemakers. There had been little attempt to control for such variables as stage of the family cycle, number and ages of children, continuous or intermittent employment or full- versus part-time work. In contrast, this study focused on a relatively homogeneous population at the point at which plans had been formulated. Thus there were a number of advantages to this design. An array of variables was explored, rather than just one factor, and both women and their husbands were included. Subjects were studied at the point at which they had made their plans, rather than years prior to or after the actual decision. Further, a relatively homogeneous population was selected, with sampling criteria, including minimal educational and occupational requirements, imposed. The purpose of these criteria was to investigate women in similar circumstances, controlling for some of the more blatant extraneous variables.

While this design has its advantages, it also presents some limitations. One concerns the time at which subjects are being questioned, i.e. before the child is born and the woman needs to act on her plans for employment. It is certainly possible that some women may change their plans after the baby's birth. However, it was believed that the decisions women make prior to the birth are an important area of study as well. Such plans may represent a more abstract or ideal notion of what each woman feels would be the best alternative and thus is an important source of information regarding this issue. Furthermore, these women were in the latter stages of pregnancy and realistically needed to have made some initial plans by that point. Indeed, as their responses indicated, most had already quit their jobs or arranged with their employers for a specific return date. In addition, as a group, they indicate that their plans are relatively definite at this time.

A more serious limitation pertains to the selection of the sample. In particular, the sampling criteria imposed limit the generalizability of results to an urban, college-educated, middle- to upper-middle-class population.

A further sampling bias resulted from the recruiting of subjects exclusively through Lamaze classes, since these classes seem to attract a certain type of population. Besides being relatively well-educated and of a relatively high socioeconomic status (both of which are consistent with the aforementioned sampling criteria), both husband and wife generally attend classes. This suggests that, as a group, the husbands are very supportive and involved in the childbirth process. Studies confirm that there are significant differences between these couples and those who choose more traditional methods of childbearing (Eustace, 1978; Oliver, 1972; Ostrum, 1972). This further limits the population to which the results of this study can be generalized.

As noted, a wide array of variables were studied. However, these can be grouped into a few types of factors. One group might be labeled external or situational factors and would include primarily demographic and occupational characteristics and practical considerations. Past research has shown that many of these variables reliably differentiate working from nonworking women, including education, income, occupation, age at childbirth and number of children. The relatively homogeneous population studied was chosen in large part to avoid such gross differences among groups. Results indicate that, in fact, all three groups were similar in regard to age, religion, marital status, occupation, number of children wanted and other characteristics.

Despite sampling criteria, however, a few such characteristics did differentiate among groups—notably women's level of education and women's income—lending additional credence to their salience. As suggested previously, the higher educational level achieved by those women planning to continue their careers would seem to be a result of the same factors (such as attitudes or career interest) that led to choosing this option.

The relationship between income and future employment plans, however, is more complex. Half of the women in this study who plan to continue full-time employment cite financial considerations as their primary motiva-tion. This is consistent with previous research indicating that financial need is generally the major reason given for women working. On the other hand, there is no difference in husband's income across groups nor does husband's or wife's income differentiate those citing financial motivations for con-tinued employment from those citing other factors.

Labor statistics indicate that husband's income is indeed related to women's employment rates but only to a certain extent. Although a woman is more likely to work as her husband's income declines, this relationship diminishes considerably at the higher income levels. In other words, at the income levels represented in this sample, labor rates are fairly stable, indicating that other factors take on greater import in women's employment plans.

In fact, it is the women's incomes that differ across groups, not the husbands'. This would seem to indicate that while critical financial need is not present, many of the women are motivated to continue working, at least in part, to maintain their current standard of living. The fact that women in the Full-time Group earn a higher percentage of the total family income would suggest that the loss of the wife's earnings would entail a greater financial sacrifice for this group.

However, other factors need to be taken into consideration in deter-mining the relationship between income and employment plans for this population. In particular, the perception of the wife's income is important and this relates in large part to attitudes toward sex roles. If the couple hold relatively traditional views, expecting the husband to be the main provider, it is likely that the wife's income, no matter how high, will be viewed as secondary and temporary, used for extras or saved. Similarly, if the couple feels very strongly that a working mother would be detrimental to a child's growth, then they would be likely to plan to live, during the children's formative years, on the husband's salary alone, even if this entails some sacrifice.

On the other hand, those couples whose attitudes are based less on sex-typed roles would be more likely to perceive themselves as a two-income family, basing consumption patterns on their combined income. When they have their first child, they may be unwilling, or unable, to reduce their standard of living, although the woman may ideally prefer to remain home and would do so if the loss of her income meant only a minor reduction in their standard of living or the accumulation of fewer savings.

Thus, when considering the effects of income (at least at this level), standard of living desired, attitudes toward the wife's earnings, intensity of beliefs about a child's needs and the degree of sacrifice the couple is willing to make all need to be taken into account. In fact, it would appear that other factors are not only involved but indeed are more relevant to this issue than the level of income per se. This conclusion is supported by the lack of differences across groups in husband's income as well as the major differences found among groups on other variables. Consistent with this are the results of the discriminant analysis which indicate that income, as well as other demographic variables, made only a minor contribution to group differentiation.

A second group of variables investigated was attitudinal factors. This would include sex-role attitudes, beliefs about the needs of a young child and the husband's attitudes toward his own roles as well as his wife's. Previous research, while inconsistent, has tended to support the hypothesis that working women hold more modern views of sex roles compared to nonworking women, i.e. they are more likely to believe that roles should not be differentiated by sex.

In the present study, many of the attitudinal variables measured showed significant differences among the three groups. Those women planning to return to work, particularly full-time, expressed a less traditional, non-differentiated view of sex roles in relation to the family sphere, compared to women planning to remain home. This was reflected both in their expressed attitudes and norms and in their actual reported behavior within their own families. Further, they had expanded their roles beyond the traditional ones of wife and mother to include a career role, although the latter was clearly secondary in importance.

Attitudes of the husbands seemed to be relatively consistent with those of their wives. Men in the Home Group expressed more traditional views regarding sex roles compared to men in the other groups and were less positive towards their wives' career roles. In addition, they themselves maintained the traditional division of roles, with career roles tending to be of primary importance to their self-identities. Men in the other groups, on the other hand, were more willing to expand their own roles and perceived their family roles as of primary importance.

The groups also differed in regard to their beliefs about the needs of a young child. Women in the Home Group strongly believed that young children need the full-time care of their mothers and that a woman who works cannot meet her family responsibilities as successfully as a full-time homemaker. In contrast, women in the Full-time Group believed that family and career responsibilities are not incompatible, even when there are young children.

These results suggest that the combination of attitudes regarding their own roles and beliefs about the needs of a young child are critical to the plans women make to continue or interrupt their careers at this stage in their lives. Women who view their roles in a relatively traditional manner and believe a child needs full-time care by the mother will be most likely to stay home. Those who view their career roles as important and do not think a child's development depends on the constant presence of the mother will be most likely to continue full-time employment. For those women who view their career roles as important but also believe that working full-time might be detrimental to their child, part-time employment, if available, would appear to be the ideal choice. If it is not available, the intensity of their beliefs, as well as other factors such as income, husband's support and career considerations would be important mediating factors. While each couple's attitudes are not as easily categorized as presented above, attitudinal factors do seem to be of primary importance to our understanding of this issue.

Personality traits were the third major group of variables investigated. Although past research in this area has shown contradictory results, it is logical to expect that women would choose among possible alternatives at least partly on the basis of their perceptions of their own needs. In this study, however, there was no relationship between the option chosen and personality traits of either the women or their husbands.

As suggested earlier, it is possible that while there are no differences among women who continue or interrupt their careers in terms of general personality traits, there may be differences in regard to the context in which these traits are expressed. A woman may fulfill a need for achievement, for example, in many spheres besides work.

However, other studies have shown differences among groups in these same personality traits. One explanation of this inconsistency may relate to the time at which various groups were studied. Earlier research investigated differences between actual working women and full-time homemakers. Perhaps the personality differences found resulted from the effects of the different options chosen rather than reflecting existing differences. Thus, personality differences would not appear in this sample since all the women had been working full-time.

The results of this study suggest, in effect, that the alternatives chosen, at this point in these women's lives, were not based on their own personality needs. The fact that the majority of women cited other motivations for their plans besides their own needs and desires is consistent with this data. However, the data is not necessarily inconsistent with those studies which have found significant personality differences between working women and homemakers and between career and homemaking oriented college women. Again, the time focus of this study would appear to be crucial. The decision to continue or interrupt her career at the birth of her first child seems to be based primarily on the individual's attitudes and expectations of herself as a woman and mother as well as her beliefs about the needs of a young child. It is probable, though, that later, when the needs of the child are not considered as demanding, differences between those women who choose to work and those who do not will be more closely related to personality differences. At this particular stage, however, other factors are of greater significance in the resolution of this issue.

Group Profiles

While each couple's plans certainly involved unique elements, the prevalence of similar variables within each group suggests that more than purely idiosyncratic factors are involved in this decision. Each of the three plans is based, at least partly, on a group of interrelated variables that are similar for most of those choosing that option and at variance with those of relevance for the other groups. Empirical support for this statement is provided by the fact that numerous variables significantly differentiated the groups as well as the results of the discriminant analysis showing that the groups could indeed be separated statistically using a combination of factors.

To better illustrate these patterns, and as a means of summarizing the results, it might be helpful to briefly profile the couples in each group, recognizing, of course, that there will be exceptions. The sketches will not be descriptive, in every respect, of all group members.

Home Group

Similar to the rest of the sample, those women planning to interrupt or terminate their careers in order to stay home and care for their first child are about 29 years old and have been married for about 3.5 years. All are college-educated but few have advanced beyond this level. They have worked full-time for almost five years and averaged $14,000 in income. Their husbands are approximately 31 years of age, have worked for about six years and earn an average of $34,000. They too are college-educated and almost half have earned graduate degrees. Both are relatively satisfied with their marriage, had planned the pregnancy and prefer that the mother remain home. Since most want at least two children and expect that they would not consider working until the child was at least three, the majority of the women expect to be full-time homemakers for at least the next five years; most plan to delay employment even longer.

The decision to stop working was a relatively easy choice for these women; they are quite certain that they will not change their minds and feel very comfortable with their plans.

This is easily understood when one recognizes their current goals and perceptions. At this stage in their lives, their focal role is that of mother and wife. As one woman wrote, "Now that I have chosen to have a family, I feel that I have consciously chosen to devote the main part of my time to my family." There is a strong identification with family roles; two-thirds rank this as most important to their self-identities.

Devoted foremost to the welfare of their children and families, women in this group perceive work as interfering with this commitment. For some, career involvement is incompatible with home obligations in general. This is well put by one woman who commented, "Marriage, not childbirth, was the time when I had to make the decision to abandon career aspirations. I had to be satisfied with just a job, i.e., a source of income and an opportunity to keep busy, but with sufficient flexibility and time to take care of husband and home." More often, however, employment is seen as interfering particularly with maternal obligations. As a group, these women strongly believe that young children need full-time care by their mothers and 88 percent indicate this is their primary reason for staying home. "I strongly feel that it is important for the development of my child emotionally, physically and socially that I be home. I don't want my child raised in a nursery school or day care. I feel healthy home life is essential in the first years of a child's life."

In general, though, the women in this group do not perceive their staying home as a sacrifice. In part, this is because their careers are of only moderate importance to them and not essential to their self-identities. It is not that they are dissatisfied with their work but rather that a career is not seen as relevant to this stage of their lives. (The majority, however, do plan to work in the future.) Further, it is expected that homemaking will be a source of satisfaction and fulfillment. "My real enjoyment of the freedom and creativity of being a housewife makes it very easy and very natural to stay home to raise our child." The lower career orientation in this group would seem to be highly related to their strong family orientations. Since career involvement and motherhood are perceived as mutually exclusive roles, at least at this point, it would be consistent for these women to avoid becoming too invested in their work roles.

The women in this group are married to men who share their values and would prefer their wives at home, not only for the child but also for themselves. As more than one woman indicated, "My husband works at a relatively high-pressure job and he prefers to have someone to come home to."

These men, while not feeling negatively toward their wives' careers, are significantly less positive than the other groups. At the same time, they are very invested in their own careers. The majority, for instance, rank their career roles as more important to their self-identities than their home roles.

Thus, the couples in this group seem to have a relatively traditional marriage and view of sex roles. While they may endorse equality in the abstract and agree that women can be as successful as men in the work world, their own lives are more or less based on the traditional gender-based division of labor. The wife's major contribution is at home, with childcare and homemaking primarily her domain. Her husband, on the other hand, sees his role as supporting the family and maintains a strong investment in his career.

Certainly, the degree to which these couples express traditional ideologies and carry them out in their own lives varies considerably and, in fact, they are probably more "liberal" than the general population. What does characterize this group fairly uniformly, though, is their strong belief in the need for full-time mothering of young children. Their motivations for staying home are based primarily on this assumption, at least consciously, while the women's perceptions of their own needs, however compatible with full-time mothering, are considered secondary.

Full-Time Group

The typical woman planning to return to work full-time was about 30 years old and had been married for about three years. She had earned a graduate degree, had been working in a relatively prestigious occupation for approximately six years, and now averaged $20,000 in income. Similarly, her thirty-one year old husband had also obtained graduate training, been working for about six years and earned an average of $24,000. Both are relatively satisfied with their marriage and their careers. The decision to return to work was not felt to be a very difficult one for these women and they indicate a fair amount of certainty about it; however, they and their husbands discussed it a great deal and the women, in particular, are only moderately comfortable with their plans. They expect, on the average, to return to their former jobs after a three-month leave of absence and most plan to hire an individual sitter to care for the baby.

While this group is far less homogeneous than the Home Group and only about a third actually prefer to work full-time, there are a number of characteristics that can be said to typify the majority of these subjects. As a whole, the women in this group, in contrast to the Home Group, have a substantial investment in their careers. They have sought advanced education which has allowed them to progress into higher level, better paying positions and their careers now provide not only monetary return but are also a source of personal satisfaction and self-identity. While the relative importance of these benefits may vary, the women in this group obtain too many advantages from their work involvement to easily give it up, even temporarily. As one woman declared, "If I were to quit work until my family is completed, I would never be able to return to the same level in the same profession and would thus sacrifice the investment of many years of education and experience, not to mention giving up the personal satisfaction that comes from being successful in my work."

This is not to imply that career involvement is more important to this group of women than their family roles. While there is more of a balance seen between the two compared to the Home Group, clear priority is still given to home roles. Perhaps one of the major differences between the two groups is that, for these women, the two roles are not perceived as incompatible. The traditional assumption that working mothers cannot establish as close and warm a relationship with their young child as a full-time homemaker is adamantly rejected by this group. While somewhat of a cliché, many women expressed the same belief that "it's the quality of time spent with the child and not the quantity." Thus, these women have sought to expand their roles, seeking satisfaction from both the traditional roles of wife and mother and their occupational involvement.

This expansion of roles to include traditionally masculine functions is consistent with their expressed sex-role attitudes. The women in this group not only highly endorse equality and non-sex-typed division of labor but have sought to implement these ideas within their own families. The majority feel that not only should their husbands be equally responsible for household tasks and childcare, but they themselves should share the job of financially supporting the family equally with their husbands. In reality, sex-linked assignments are still quite evident in this group but less so in comparison to the rest of the sample.

There is a high degree of support offered by the husbands of these women. They have very positive feelings about their wives' careers and share similar attitudes regarding sex roles and the ability of women to simultaneously combine family and career involvement. Further, they too have begun to expand their traditional roles and the majority now perceive family roles as contributing most to their sense of personal identity. Thus, the couples in this group have moved away from the traditional division of labor toward a greater mutual sharing of roles.

Despite their expressed attitudes, the women in this group are to some extent uncomfortable with their plans. Deeply rooted norms are not easily abandoned; further, prevailing social attitudes have not changed to the extent of wholeheartedly supporting a mother's choice to work. Thus, many of the women indicate that they would prefer not to work full-time but need the additional income. As already discussed, this seems to be a reflection not only of perceived financial need and rising expectations regarding desired lifestyle, but it is also a more socially and personally acceptable motivation.

However, evidence also suggests that the Full-time Group is composed of at least two subgroups, identified by their ideal preferences. The major subgroup is best characterized by the description given above and cite personal and career considerations as primary motivations for employment. Even in this subgroup, though, economic factors are quite relevant to their plans.

The women who indicate that they would prefer to remain home cite financial motivations as primary. Although they are less invested in their careers as a source of identity and are more likely to be concerned about the effects of their dual role-involvement on the child, compared to the other members of this group, they are not as traditional in their attitudes toward familial roles as women in the Home Group. The small size of this subgroup in the present sample makes it difficult to really identify valid patterns although hypotheses were offered in the previous section. Certainly, further research, with larger samples of women working despite their conscious preferences, is needed.

Part-time Group

Women in this sample who were planning to return to work part-time were, on the average, 29 years old, had been married for 3.5 years, worked for six years and earned about $16,000. They were as likely as not to have attended graduate school. Their husbands were about 31 years of age, had worked for eight years and earned approximately $36,000. About two-thirds had attended graduate school. Both spouses were highly satisfied with their marriage and relatively satisfied with their careers.

The decision to work part-time resulted only after a great deal of discussion with friends and colleagues, and these women are still not completely certain that they will actually carry out their plans. Perhaps part of the uncertainty is related to the fact that almost half of these women had unplanned pregnancies. These factors would seem to reflect some degree of conflict regarding parenting and career roles.

Like the Full-time Group, these women manifest an interest and investment in their careers. While family roles are clearly more important, their work roles offer personal satisfaction and, secondarily, economic rewards. Unlike the Full-time Group, however, they are not sure that a substantial career involvement would not interfere with good mothering, although they are not as likely as the Home Group to believe that dual roles are necessarily incompatible. As one woman commented, "I'm not sure how well I will adapt to staying home, but I haven't the energy for a full-time career and babies." In other words, their assumptions regarding a child's needs as well as their conceptions of their own needs and responsibilities as individuals and women are not completely defined and are no doubt in the midst of change. Thus, these women are faced with conflictual feelings. They do not want to interrupt their careers, but they are concerned about their child. Maintaining a part-time involvement in their careers seems like a perfect solution to this dilemma; without having to entirely give up the benefits of work, they can still remain home much of the time, giving their child primary attention. This view was expressed by one woman who wrote, "It is important to understand that in a free-lance situation my schedule will be very flexible. Each job that I accept will have its own deadline and I will be able to work it into the schedule the baby and I have established. I am fortunate that my line of work will allow me to complete most of my work at home."

Others may not be as fortunate. It is likely that some of the women in the other groups faced similar conflicts but did not have the option of working part-time. This is reflected in the fact that part-time work was the most chosen ideal preference for this sample as well as for others (Hall and Gordon, 1973).

The husbands in this group are generally quite supportive of their wives' work roles and do not feel that this involvement will interfere with meeting the needs of the child or their own needs. They also view their own family roles as primary, although they are not as committed as the men in the Full-time Group to sharing traditional roles in their own lives. Perhaps these men, like their wives, feel some confusion and conflict regarding sex roles. Despite their ambivalence, however, they do support their wives' plans and, in fact, probably even encourage them. As one man wrote, "My wife wasn't comfortable with the idea of leaving our baby with someone else for the whole day but there were too many positive aspects to her work to give it up entirely. She was fortunately able to work something out with her boss so that she could bring some of her work home and have a much reduced schedule at the office. I think she will be much happier being able to get away from the house for at least part of the week."

It is probable that, for these women, their husbands' attitudes are particularly critical. Because of their own ambivalence, the husband's encouragement, or lack of it, may be one of the deciding factors in this decision. If her husband is against her working, it is quite likely that she will postpone employment. On the other hand, if her husband feels positively about her working, it is likely that he will be able to reduce her apprehensions.

While working part-time may be seen as "the best of both worlds," there is some evidence that women in this group remain quite ambivalent about their roles. Perhaps this is because part-time work, in effect, is an incomplete resolution of their internal conflict, allowing them to avoid choosing between working full-time or not working at all. Perhaps it is because, more than in any other group, this decision is perceived as a personal choice based on their own needs. For whatever reason, it seems particuarly difficult for these women to relinquish their traditional roles, particularly childcare. As noted previously, despite the fact that a large proportion of the husbands will be caring for the baby while their wives work, the women are less likely to feel that childcare should be shared. One might hypothesize that choosing to work is likely to make a mother feel guilty and, to compensate, she attempts to be a "superwoman." Unfortunately, this has a number of implications: in particular, it is likely to lead to conflicts and role overload.

In Regard to Changing Values

It was expected that one of the byproducts of this study would be to further our understanding of the degree to which changing values and attitudes have affected a college-educated population. It would appear that most of these women and men strongly endorse sexual equality in the abstract. However, there has been considerably less acceptance of these ideals in the couples' own lives; clearly, changes in behavior have lagged behind changes in attitude.

In particular, the primacy of motherhood is widely accepted. While the view of family roles as the be-all and end-all for women is generally rejected, the idea that these roles should be a woman's main priority is not. Only a small percentage of women in this sample prefer to return to work full-time at this point. Even among those who endorse equal sharing of many traditional roles, childcare was more likely to be seen as a woman's responsibility and those women who planned to maintain dual roles indicated that they were indeed somewhat uncomfortable with these plans. (While it should be noted that most of the men also felt their family roles were most salient, there was greater variation here. In addition, only one or two indicated that they perceived any conflict between their family and occupational interests.) As previously noted, this seems to be a reflection not only of perceived social norms but also of deep-seated assumptions regarding motherhood.

Perhaps this has to do with the nature of these roles. Motherhood can best be understood as an ascribed role, attained because of one's inherent characteristics (e.g., gender) or implicit relationship to another. That is, once a woman has a child, she is a mother regardless of her future behavior. This is in contrast to an achieved role which is reached primarily through personal behavior or election. While achieved roles are evaluated on a range from neutral to highly positive, evaluations of ascribed roles range from highly negative to neutral (Darley, 1976). Thus, there may be little social reward for being a good parent, and failure to meet expectations is judged severely. In the past, career achievement for women has implied poor performance as a mother, since the two roles were viewed as incompatible. While this view may be changing to some extent, it is still widely assumed that a good mother remains home with her preschool child. In addition, the parent role has always been a particularly salient one for women. Therefore, it is very difficult for most women to work at this time without feeling some concern that they are failing as mothers.

Perhaps the traditional assumption that is most critical in this regard concerns the belief that young children require exclusive care from their mothers to develop in a healthy manner. Despite the fact that there is little evidence that children of working mothers fare any worse than children of homemakers (Hoffman, 1974; Zambrana, et al., 1979), this conviction has been widely circulated and accepted by American society. Those who believe this most strongly (in this sample, the Home Group) also seem to accept many of the other traditional assumptions and plan their lives accordingly; that is, they do not invest themselves psychologically in their careers.

On the other hand, there seems to be some evidence that this assumption is being more widely questioned. However, even those who most strongly reject this tenet indicate that lingering doubt remains. This is certainly understandable; while one might doubt that working will be detrimental to a child, it is difficult to risk this possibility. Thus this assumption is quite binding on women and, as has been previously suggested, has negative implications for women's career development.

Thus, the extent to which values and assumptions regarding sex-roles have changed is only moderate. While many question the veracity of these norms, few are willing to commit themselves to changes in their own lives. In particular, the concepts regarding a young child's needs remain a critical barrier to changing sex roles.

A Comment on the Question of Choice

Certainly, reasons for employment as well as career interruption are multifaceted. As suggested earlier, there is rarely only a single motivating force involved in this decision; rather the combination of perceived benefits and costs to the woman, her child and her husband need to be weighed by each couple before a decision can be reached.

However, the primary reasons given by subjects for their plans are quite revealing. In particular, it is interesting to note that few women cite their own desires as their major motivation. It is not clear whether women simply do not give preference to their own needs or whether they are generally unwilling to admit it. Certainly the fact that personality differences among the groups were not salient supports the former hypothesis. Rather, primary motivations given often reflect family needs. Women in the Home Group stay home primarily for their child, while many of the women in the Full-time Group work primarily because their families need the income. Only women in the Part-time Group acknowledge that their plans are based primarily on their own needs. The consequences of "choosing" to work, even part-time, have already been suggested. It may be that it is easier and less conflictual for women to avoid, in some manner, the necessity of making a genuine choice. Bailyn's essay (1964) explores quite well the difficulties that such a choice entails for women.

While it might seem ideal if all women (and men) could choose the combination of work and family involvement that best used their energies and capabilites and provided the most personal satisfaction, this might also have the effect of reducing women's roles both at home and at work from significant societal contributions to something akin to a hobby. For example, the element of choice that is often perceived to be attached to women's work-roles seems to not only increase intrapsychic conflict but also makes it difficult for a woman's career commitment to be taken seriously. It would be interesting to know how the majority of men would respond to a question regarding their motivation for work. While one might expect money to be the primary motive cited, the fact that men are rarely perceived as having a genuine choice enables them to make work an integral part of their lives with little hesitation or conflict. On the other hand, if homemakers were perceived as choosing their lifestyles based primarily on their own needs rather than the needs of their families, it might be very difficult for a woman, given the persistence of the Protestant Ethic, to not work. Understood in this framework, motivations cited for these women's plans are much more easily comprehensible.

Some Further Implications

There are a number of relevant implications of this study. Perhaps the most critical relates to the fact that a major difference between women who plan to continue employment and those who interrupt their careers at the birth of the first child is their perception of the needs of their child. This issue has been discussed in previous sections. However, one of the implications of this would seem to be that if occupational involvement were not perceived as incompatible with good mothering, career commitment among women would be greatly enhanced. Clearly, there is an urgent need for research in this area. While negative effects of working on children have not been empirically supported, few studies of infants have been undertaken. Thus it is not really known what the critical factors are in this regard. Such information is significant not only to assist women in planning their lives but also to alleviate the doubt and anxiety experienced by millions of working mothers.

Another significant implication involves the nature of men's roles in contemporary society. Whether a woman works or not, and to what extent, is closely related to not only her husband's attitudes toward her career but, perhaps even more importantly, to the saliency of and investment in his own roles. It would seem that for women to be able to satisfactorily expand their roles, their husbands need to do likewise. In particular, a change in the traditional concept of a career as requiring single-minded devotion that is held by many men, as well as employers, is necessary. At the same time, there needs to be an increased opportunity for men to become more involved in their family roles and to experience both personal satisfaction and societal rewards from this involvement. This will not be an easy task, as there is a strong attachment to traditional sex-linked expectations not only by men but also by their wives. It seems particularly difficult for women to feel completely comfortable giving up some of their childcare responsibilities.

For many women, part-time employment appears to be a panacea for the conflict between family and career roles. As such, it would be important to expand part-time job opportunities for women. While this is often the most preferred choice, it may ultimately lead to dissatisfaction and frustration due particularly to role overload. As Rossi (1965) suggests, part-time employment may "avoid a more basic change in the relations between men and women, a means whereby, with practically no change in the man's role and minimal change in the woman's, she can continue to be the same wife and mother she's been in the past" (p. 53). Perhaps what is needed then are more part-time opportunities, or at least more flexible work situations, not only for women, but also for men.

Directions for Future Research

While there are numerous aspects related to women's dual roles which should be addressed in future research, the results of this investigation suggest several specific avenues for study. Certainly, follow-up studies of couples several months after childbirth would be important to determine if the plans made during pregnancy were, in fact, implemented and if not, what factors led to the changes in these plans.

Further, replication of this study with other populations would be useful. In particular, women with varying degrees of education, incomes and types of occupation may weigh the same factors quite differently in formulating their plans.

It would also be interesting to explore which variables are related to the decision to work or not at other points in time, e.g. when children are school-age. It is certainly possible that the factors which relate to women choosing employment or full-time homemaking change at different stages in their lives.

Investigations concerning those women who work part-time are also needed. This study indicates that this group is, in many ways, distinct from those women who plan to work full-time as well as from those who plan no immediate employment. Past research then which has included this group in either of the other two would seem to be based on erroneous assumptions. In addition, since so many women seem to prefer a part-time career involvement, it would be important to investigate the ramifications of this option.

Finally, the importance of the husband's perceptions of his own and his wife's roles have been shown to be quite relevant. Future research which addresses the role of the husband in this area is clearly needed.

Conclusion

The purpose of this study was to determine which factors were related to women's plans to interrupt or continue their careers, full- or part-time, at the birth of their first child. While this decision involved the weighing, for each couple, of a complex and multifaceted group of factors, similarities among couples and differences among groups were apparent in regard to a number of variables. These included wife's education and income, expressed motivations for plans, sex-role attitudes of both husband and wife, the relative importance of roles to each spouse and the husband's attitude towards his wife's career. Personality differences among groups, however, were not found.

The results of this study suggest, however, that the most salient factors were attitudinal. That is, individual personality needs and external factors were less pertinent to this issue, at least for this population, than the women's perceptions of the appropriate roles for themselves as women and their beliefs about the needs of their child.

This is not to suggest that these women were generally making plans that were in opposition to their perceived needs; for the most part, their own needs were seen as compatible with, although often secondary to, their self-expectations. It is also not meant to imply that the plans women make regarding career and family are related only to this dimension. However, the results do suggest the tremendous significance of social views and the degree to which couples accept alternative ideologies. If we hope then to continue to offer expanding options to both women and men, it is imperative that we address these ideological issues.

Appendix A

Preliminary Information Sheet

The purpose of this study is to look at some of the factors that may be involved in a woman's plans to continue or interrupt her career at the birth of her first child. If you are in a profession or have been developing a career and you and your husband would be willing to participate in this study, please complete the following information. You will each be given a questionnaire to complete which you may return to me at your next class meeting. All responses are strictly confidential; statistics complied will not identify individuals in any way whatsoever.

If you do not wish to participate, I would appreciate it if you would still fill out the information below.

Thank you very much for your cooperation.

> Debra Behrman
> Northwestern University

1. Will this be your first child? _____ Yes _____ No

2. Child's Expected Birthdate? _____

3. Wife's Occupation (please be as specific as possible)

4. Wife's Level of Education and Degrees Obtained:

5. Are you (wife) currently (or were you prior to pregnancy)
   _____ Working full-time
   _____ Working part-time
   _____ Not working outside the home
   _____ Attending school
   _____ Other (please explain) _____

6. After your child is born, what are your plans regarding work?
   _____ Return to work full-time within _____ months. Hrs. per week? _____
   _____ Return to work part-time within _____ months. Hrs. per week? _____
   _____ No plans to return to work until my child is at least _____ years old
   _____ I have not decided yet, but will do so before baby is born
   _____ I have not decided yet; will wait to see what happens after baby is born
   _____ Other (please explain) _____

7. Husband's Occupation (please be as specific as possible)

8.   Husband's Level of Education and Degrees Obtained:

9.   Would you be willing to participate in this study by completing a questionnaire?
        _____ Yes
        _____ No

Research Consent Form

I understand that:

1.   I am being asked to participate in a study investigating some of the factors involved in a woman's plans to interrupt or continue her career at the birth of her first child.

2.   Participation in this study is completely voluntary and I may withdraw my consent at any time.

3.   If I agree to participate, I will be asked to complete a questionnaire. The questionnaire will ask about my future plans regarding employment, factors related to these plans, my attitudes about roles in society and my personality characteristics.

4.   Information furnished by me will be completely confidential; statistics compiled from this study will not identify me personally in any way.

I have read the above and have had my questions answered to my satisfaction.

    I agree to participate in this study.

                                        Signed _____
                                        Date _____

Appendix B

Wife's Questionnaire

Dear Participant,

Thank you for agreeing to participate in this study of women and their husbands who are having their first child. As explained, the study is an attempt to investigate what factors influence women like yourself to plan to either continue or interrupt their careers after their child is born. As a woman with a career and a future mother, your thoughts and concerns about this decision are a valuable source of information that can contribute to our understanding of some of the issues and concerns that many women in our society face today.

The attached questionnaire asks about your future plans, your beliefs about the role of women and men in today's society and your personal characteristics. Please be assured that your responses will be kept completely confidential. While each individual is very important, findings will report overall patterns of response and not single out individuals.

I hope that you will find time to complete the questionnaire in the next week and return it to me at your next class meeting. Full and complete responses from all those who agreed to participate is important for the accuracy of this study. If you have any questions at all, please feel free to call me at 743-6705 (evenings.)

Thank you for your cooperation and your time.

Sincerely,

Debra Behrman

Debra Behrman
Northwestern University

INSTRUCTIONS

The following questions are of a few basic types. In most
cases, and unless otherwise indicated, you are asked to circle
the number of the response that best applies for you. For other
questions, a brief written response is required. A third type
asks you to rank order a set of statements.

While the questionnaire may seem rather long, most of it
requires only brief answers and goes very quickly. Your
responses will be kept strictly confidential.

Please answer all items as frankly as possible. We are
interested in what you think; please don't ask others for
their opinions.

Thank you.

Date _____

<u>BACKGROUND INFORMATION</u>

1. YOUR AGE _____   2. HUSBAND'S AGE _____

3. WHAT IS YOUR MARITAL STATUS?

        1. Married   4. Divorced
        2. Remarried   5. Widowed
        3. Separated

4. HOW LONG HAVE YOU BEEN MARRIED? _____

5. WHAT IS YOUR RACE?

        1. Caucasian   3. Hispanic
        2. Black   4. Other (please specify) _____

6. WHAT IS YOUR RELIGION?

        1. Protestant   4. None
        2. Catholic   5. Other (please specify) _____
        3. Jewish

7. WHAT IS YOUR LEVEL OF EDUCATION?

        a. Highest grade completed (please circle)

               High School   College   Graduate School
               9 10 11 12   1 2 3 4   1 2 3 4 5 6

        b. Degrees obtained; specialized training received, etc.

        _____

8. WHAT IS YOUR PRESENT OCCUPATION? (please be specific)

9. BEFORE YOUR PREGNANCY, WERE YOU

        1. Working full-time   Hours per week? _____
        2. Working part-time   Hours per week? _____
        3. Student   Full-time ___ Part-time ___ Degree sought ___
        4. Not employed but looking for work
        5. Not employed
        6. Other (please explain) _____

10. NUMBER OF YEARS AT OCCUPATION _____

11. YOUR INCOME (not including husband's) If not currently working, what was
     your income from your last job? _____

12. WHAT IS YOUR EMPLOYER'S POLICY REGARDING MATERNITY LEAVE?

13. HOW FLEXIBLE IS YOUR CURRENT JOB (or last held job) IN TERMS OF WORK SCHEDULE?

      very   somewhat   not at all
       1   2   3   4   5

14. WHAT IS YOUR HUSBAND'S LEVEL OF EDUCATION?

a. Highest grade completed

High School	College	Graduate School
9 10 11 12	1 2 3 4	1 2 3 4 5 6 7 8

b. Degrees obtained; specialized training received, etc.

_____

15. WHAT IS YOUR HUSBAND'S PRESENT OCCUPATION? (please be specific)

16. BEFORE YOUR PREGNANCY, WAS YOUR HUSBAND

1. Working full-time   Hours per week? _____
2. Working part-time   Hours per week? _____
3. Student   Full-time ___ Part-time ___ Degree sought _____
4. Not employed but looking for work
5. Not employed
6. Other (please explain) _____

17. IF YOUR HUSBAND'S EMPLOYMENT STATUS HAS CHANGED SINCE YOUR PREGNANCY, PLEASE EXPLAIN

18. HUSBAND'S NUMBER OF YEARS AT OCCUPATION _____

19. HUSBAND'S INCOME _____

20. DOES YOUR HUSBAND'S EMPLOYER HAVE ANY POLICY REGARDING PATERNITY LEAVE?

21. HOW FLEXIBLE IS YOUR HUSBAND'S JOB IN TERMS OF WORK SCHEDULE?

very		somewhat		not at all
1	2	3	4	5

22. WHAT IS YOUR CHILD'S EXPECTED BIRTHDATE? _____

23. THE PREGNANCY WAS

1. planned
2. unplanned

24. HOW MANY CHILDREN WOULD YOU LIKE TO HAVE? _____

FUTURE PLANS

1. AFTER THE BIRTH OF YOUR BABY, WHAT ARE YOUR PLANS REGARDING EMPLOYMENT?

1. Return to work full-time
2. Return to work part-time
3. Attend school   full-time _____ part-time _____   degree sought _____
4. No plans to return to work during the first year
5. I have not decided yet, but will do so before baby is born
6. I have not decided yet; will wait to see what happens after baby is born
7. Other (please explain) _____

2. HOW DEFINITE ARE YOUR PLANS?

    1. Very definite; all arrangements have been made
    2. Pretty definite
    3. Somewhat definite; details need to be worked out
    4. Not very definite
    5. Not at all definite; I really haven't made any arrangements

3. HOW CERTAIN DO YOU FEEL THAT YOU WILL ACTUALLY CARRY OUT THESE PLANS?

    1. Very certain that this is what I will do
    2. Pretty certain
    3. Fairly certain but I am open to changes if it doesn't work out later
    4. Not very certain
    5. Not at all certain; I really don't know what I will actually do

4. AFTER THE BIRTH OF YOUR BABY, WHAT ARE YOUR HUSBAND'S PLANS REGARDING EMPLOYMENT?

    1. Work full-time   Hours per week? _____
    2. Work part-time   Hours per week? _____
    3. Attend school   Full-time ___ Part-time ___ Degree sought _____
    4. No plans to return to work during the first year
    5. He has not decided yet; will do so before baby is born
    6. He has not decided yet; will wait to see what happens after baby is born
    7. Other (please explain) _____

IF YOU PLAN TO RETURN TO WORK FULL-TIME PLEASE COMPLETE THE FOLLOWING QUESTIONS

5. HOW SOON DO YOU PLAN TO RETURN TO WORK? _____

6. NUMBER OF HOURS PER WEEK _____

7. TIME OF DAY YOU PLAN TO WORK _____

8. HOW FLEXIBLE WILL YOUR WORK SCHEDULE BE?

    very   somewhat   not at all
    1   2   3   4   5

9. ARE YOU PLANNING TO RETURN TO YOUR CURRENT JOB?

    1. Yes
    2. No

10. IF YOU ARE PLANNING TO RETURN TO YOUR CURRENT JOB, WHAT ARRANGEMENTS HAVE YOU MADE WITH YOUR EMPLOYER?

11. IF NOT PLANNING TO RETURN TO YOUR CURRENT JOB, PLEASE EXPLAIN:

12. WHAT ARRANGEMENTS HAVE YOU MADE OR PLAN TO MAKE REGARDING CHILD-CARE?

IF YOU PLAN TO RETURN TO WORK PART-TIME, PLEASE COMPLETE THE FOLLOWING QUESTIONS

13. HOW SOON DO YOU PLAN TO RETURN TO WORK? _____

14. NUMBER OF HOURS PER WEEK? _____

15. TIME OF DAY YOU PLAN TO WORK? _____

16. HOW FLEXIBLE WILL YOUR WORK SCHEDULE BE?

    very   somewhat   not at all
     1   2   3   4   5

17. ARE YOU PLANNING TO RETURN TO YOUR CURRENT JOB?

    1. Yes
    2. No

18. IF YES, WHAT ARRANGEMENTS HAVE YOU MADE WITH YOUR EMPLOYER?

19. IF NOT, PLEASE EXPLAIN

20. WHAT ARRANGEMENTS HAVE YOU MADE OR PLAN TO MAKE REGARDING CHILD-CARE?

21. DO YOU PLAN TO RETURN TO WORK FULL-TIME IN THE FUTURE?

    1. Yes
    2. No
    3. I don't know

22. HOW OLD WOULD YOUR BABY HAVE TO BE BEFORE YOU CONSIDERED WORKING FULL-TIME? _____

IF YOU DO NOT PLAN TO RETURN TO WORK DURING THE FIRST YEAR, PLEASE COMPLETE THE FOLLOWING

23. HAVE YOU STOPPED WORKING YET?

    1. Yes. I stopped working _____ months into my pregnancy
    2. No.   I plan to stop working _____ months into my pregnancy.

24. ARE YOU PLANNING TO RETURN TO WORK SOMETIME IN THE FUTURE?

    1. Yes
    2. No
    3. I don't know

25. IF YES, HOW OLD WOULD YOUR CHILD HAVE TO BE BEFORE YOU CONSIDERED WORKING? _____

IF YOU HAVE NOT YET DECIDED WHAT TO DO REGARDING EMPLOYMENT DURING YOUR CHILD'S
FIRST YEAR, PLEASE COMPLETE THE FOLLOWING:

26. AT THIS TIME, ARE YOU LEANING MORE TOWARDS:

    1. Returning to work full-time
    2. Returning to work part-time
    3. No employment outside the home
    4. Other (please explain) _____

27. WHAT ARRANGEMENTS, IF ANY, HAVE YOU MADE WITH YOUR EMPLOYER?

<u>FOR EVERYONE</u>

   IF YOU FEEL YOUR PLANS WERE NOT ADEQUATELY EXPLAINED ON THE ABOVE QUESTIONS,
   PLEASE FEEL FREE TO ADD ANY ADDITIONAL INFORMATION BELOW.

FACTORS RELATED TO PLANS

1. HOW EASY OR DIFFICULT HAS IT BEEN FOR YOU TO DECIDE WHAT YOU PLANNED TO DO REGARDING RETURNING TO WORK OR REMAINING HOME WITH YOUR CHILD?

    1. Very easy; I knew exactly what I was going to do
    2. Pretty easy
    3. Neither easy nor difficult; I had an idea about what I was going to do but was not completely certain
    4. Pretty difficult
    5. Very difficult; I experienced a lot of conflict in making this decision

2. HOW COMFORTABLE OR UNCOMFORTABLE DO YOU FEEL ABOUT YOUR PLANS?

    1. Very comfortable; I think I'll be very satisfied
    2. Pretty comfortable
    3. Both comfortable and uncomfortable; there's no perfect plan
    4. Pretty uncomfortable
    5. Very uncomfortable; I think I'll feel very dissatisfied

3. WHOSE DECISION IS IT, YOURS OR YOUR HUSBAND'S?

    1. My decision totally
    2. More my decision than my husband's
    3. Joint decision
    4. More my husband's decision than mine

4. HOW MUCH HAVE YOU AND YOUR HUSBAND DISCUSSED THIS ISSUE?

a great deal		some		not at all
1	2	3	4	5

5. WAS THERE ANY DISAGREEMENT BETWEEN YOU ABOUT THIS ISSUE?

a great deal		some		none at all
1	2	3	4	5

6. WHAT DO YOU THINK YOUR HUSBAND WOULD PREFER YOU TO DO WITHIN THE NEXT YEAR AFTER YOUR BABY IS BORN?

    1. Return to work full-time
    2. Return to work part-time
    3. Not work outside the home
    4. No preference
    5. Other (Please explain) _____

7. WHAT WOULD YOU PREFER YOUR HUSBAND DO AFTER YOUR BABY IS BORN?

    1. Work full-time
    2. Work part-time
    3. Not work outside the home
    4. No preference
    5. Other (Please explain) _____

8. DID YOU DISCUSS THIS ISSUE AND YOUR PLANS WITH ANY OF THE FOLLOWING?
   (Please circle all that apply)

   1. Parents
   2. Other family members
   3. Friends
   4. Colleagues
   5. Professional consultants (clergy, psychologists, educators, etc.)
   6. Other (please specify) _____

9. HOW MUCH INFLUENCE DID EACH OF THE FOLLOWING HAVE ON YOUR DECISION?

	None		Some		A great deal
1. Parents	1	2	3	4	5
2. Other family members	1	2	3	4	5
3. Friends	1	2	3	4	5
4. Colleagues	1	2	3	4	5
5. Professional consultants	1	2	3	4	5
6. Other	1	2	3	4	5

10. PLEASE RANK IN ORDER OF IMPORTANCE (NUMBER 1 BEING MOST IMPORTANT) WHICHEVER
    OF THE FOLLOWING ARE YOUR MAJOR REASONS FOR YOUR PLANS

    _____ Financial considerations
    _____ Needs of my child
    _____ Practical considerations (e.g. child-care, flexibility of hours, etc.)
    _____ My own needs and desires
    _____ Career considerations
    _____ My husband's needs and desires
    _____ Available job opportunities

11. HOW IMPORTANT ARE EACH OF THESE FACTORS IN YOUR DECISION?

	Very imp't		Somewhat imp't		Not imp't
1. Financial considerations	1	2	3	4	5
2. Needs of my child	1	2	3	4	5
3. Practical considerations	1	2	3	4	5
4. My own needs and desires	1	2	3	4	5
5. Career considerations	1	2	3	4	5
6. My husband's needs and desires	1	2	3	4	5
7. Available job opportunities	1	2	3	4	5

12. IF THERE ARE OTHER FACTORS THAT WERE INVOLVED IN YOUR DECISION THAT ARE NOT
    INCLUDED IN THE ABOVE, PLEASE DESCRIBE BELOW.

13. IN TERMS OF JUST YOUR OWN PERSONAL NEEDS AND DESIRES, DISREGARDING FINANCIAL CONCERNS, YOUR HUSBAND'S PREFERENCES, AND YOUR IDEAS ABOUT THE NEEDS OF A YOUNG CHILD, WHAT WOULD YOU PREFER TO DO REGARDING EMPLOYMENT DURING YOUR CHILD'S FIRST YEAR?

    1. Return to work full-time
    2. Return to work part-time
    3. Not work outside the home at all
    4. Attend school
    5. Other (Please explain) _____

14. EVERYONE HAS A VARIETY OF DIFFERENT ROLES IN LIFE (e.g. SPOUSE, WORKER, FRIEND, etc.) THESE CAN BE DIVIDED INTO ROUGHLY THREE MAJOR AREAS: CAREER OR WORK ROLES, HOME AND FAMILY ROLES AND PERSONAL ROLES. HOW IMPORTANT ARE EACH OF THESE TO YOUR PERSONAL IDENTITY?

		Very imp't		Somewhat imp't		Not imp't
1.	Career or work roles	1	2	3	4	5
2.	Home and family roles	1	2	3	4	5
3.	Personal roles	1	2	3	4	5

15. PLEASE RANK THE IMPORTANCE OF THESE ROLES TO YOU WITH NUMBER 1 BEING MOST IMPORTANT

    _____ Career or work roles
    _____ Home and family roles
    _____ Personal roles

16. HOW IMPORTANT DO YOU THINK YOUR HUSBAND'S ROLES ARE TO HIM?

		Very imp't		Somewhat imp't		Not imp't
1.	Career or work roles	1	2	3	4	5
2.	Home and family roles	1	2	3	4	5
3.	Personal roles	1	2	3	4	5

17. PLEASE RANK THESE ROLES IN TERMS OF THE IMPORTANCE YOU THINK THEY HAVE TO YOUR HUSBAND (WITH NUMBER 1 BEING MOST IMPORTANT)

    _____ Career or work roles
    _____ Home and family roles
    _____ Personal roles

18. HOW DO YOU THINK YOUR HUSBAND FEELS ABOUT YOUR CAREER?

    1. Very positive; he very much likes the idea of my having a career
    2. Somewhat positive
    3. Neutral; he doesn't care one way or the other
    4. Somewhat negative
    5. Very negative; he would much prefer that I not have a career at all

19. HOW SUPPORTIVE HAS YOUR HUSBAND BEEN OF YOUR CAREER PURSUITS UP TO NOW?

    1. Unconditional and active support
    2. Unconditional but inactive support
    3. Conditional support
    4. Resigned to it
    5. Has actively discouraged it

20. OVERALL, HOW SATISFIED OR DISSATISFIED HAVE YOU BEEN WITH YOUR CAREER TO DATE?

Very satisfied		Neutral		Very dissatisfied
1	2	3	4	5

21. OVERALL, HOW SATISFIED OR DISSATISFIED HAVE YOU BEEN WITH YOUR MARRIAGE TO DATE?

Very satisfied		Neutral		Very dissatisfied
1	2	3	4	5

22. OVERALL, HOW SATISFIED OR DISSATISFIED DO YOU THINK YOUR HUSBAND HAS BEEN WITH HIS CAREER TO DATE?

Very satisfied		Neutral		Very dissatisfied
1	2	3	4	5

23. OVERALL, HOW SATISFIED OR DISSATISFIED DO YOU THINK YOUR HUSBAND HAS BEEN WITH YOUR MARRIAGE TO DATE?

Very satisfied		Neutral		Very dissatisfied
1	2	3	4	5

24. HERE IS A LIST OF THINGS A PERSON COULD HAVE ON HER JOB. HOW IMPORTANT HAVE EACH OF THE FOLLOWING BEEN TO YOU ON YOUR JOB?

	Not very Important			Moderately Important		Extremely Important	
1. The amount of pay you get	1	2	3	4	5	6	7
2. The quality of the equipment you work with	1	2	3	4	5	6	7
3. Your chances of getting a promotion	1	2	3	4	5	6	7
4. The physical surroundings on your job	1	2	3	4	5	6	7
5. The chances you have to accomplish something worthwhile	1	2	3	4	5	6	7
6. The chances you have to learn new things	1	2	3	4	5	6	7
7. The chances you have to do something that makes you feel good about yourself as a person	1	2	3	4	5	6	7
8. The chances you have to do the things that you do best	1	2	3	4	5	6	7
9. The chances you have to do a variety of different things	1	2	3	4	5	6	7
10. The friendliness of the people you work with	1	2	3	4	5	6	7
11. The way your supervisor treats you	1	2	3	4	5	6	7
12. The respect you receive from the people you work with	1	2	3	4	5	6	7
13. Your fringe benefits	1	2	3	4	5	6	7
14. The opportunity to think about other things besides your work	1	2	3	4	5	6	7
15. The opportunity to develop your skills and abilities	1	2	3	4	5	6	7
16. The freedom to talk with people on the job	1	2	3	4	5	6	7
17. The chances you have to move around during your working day	1	2	3	4	5	6	7

25. WHO DO YOU THINK SHOULD BE RESPONSIBLE FOR PROVIDING FOR A FAMILY FINANCIALLY?

1. Mainly wife
2. Wife more than husband
3. Wife and husband equally
4. Husband more than wife
5. Mainly husband

26. WHO DO YOU THINK SHOULD BE RESPONSIBLE FOR HOUSEHOLD TASKS?

1. Mainly wife
2. Wife more than husband
3. Wife and husband equally
4. Husband more than wife
5. Mainly husband

27. WHO PERFORMS HOUSEHOLD TASKS NOW?

1. Mainly wife
2. Wife more than husband
3. Wife and husband equally
4. Husband more than wife
5. Mainly husband

28. WHO DO YOU THINK SHOULD BE RESPONSIBLE FOR CARE OF AN INFANT?

    1. Mainly wife
    2. Wife more than husband
    3. Wife and husband equally

    4. Husband more than wife
    5. Mainly husband

29. AFTER YOUR BABY IS BORN, WHO DO YOU THINK WILL BE RESPONSIBLE FOR HIS OR HER CARE?

    1. Mainly wife
    2. Wife more than husband
    3. Wife and husband equally

    4. Husband more than wife
    5. Mainly husband

30. AFTER YOUR BABY IS BORN, WHO DO YOU THINK WILL PERFORM HOUSEHOLD TASKS?

    1. Mainly wife
    2. Wife more than husband
    3. Wife and husband equally

    4. Husband more than wife
    5. Mainly husband

31. IN YOUR OPINION, FOR A MOTHER TO BE EMPLOYED BY CHOICE (NOT DUE TO FINANCIAL NECESSITY) HER ONLY OR YOUNGEST CHILD SHOULD BE AT LEAST

    1. Six months or less
    2. Six months to a year
    3. One to two years

    4. Two to three years
    5. Three to five years
    6. School-age or older

32. GIVE YOUR ESTIMATE OF WHAT YOUR HUSBAND WOULD SAY TO THE ABOVE QUESTION

    1. Six months or less
    2. Six months to a year
    3. One to two years

    4. Two to three years
    5. Three to five years
    6. School-age or older

33. GIVE YOUR ESTIMATE OF WHAT YOUR MOTHER WOULD SAY TO THE ABOVE QUESTION

    1. Six months or less
    2. Six months to a year
    3. One to two years

    4. Two to three years
    5. Three to five years
    6. School-age or older

34. THE PREVAILING SOCIAL VIEW IN THE U.S. WOULD SAY THAT THE AGE OF THE CHILD IN THE ABOVE CASE SHOULD BE:

    1. Six months or less
    2. Six months to a year
    3. One to two years

    4. Two to three years
    5. Three to five years
    6. School-age or older

35. HOW BOTHERED WOULD YOU BE IF ANY OF THE FOLLOWING OCCURRED DURING THE NEXT YEAR?

		Very		Somewhat		Not at all
1.	Not having enough time to spend with my child as I would like	1	2	3	4	5
2.	Not having enough time together with my husband as I would like	1	2	3	4	5
3.	Not having enough time to devote to my career as I would like	1	2	3	4	5
4.	Negative attitudes of others towards working mothers	1	2	3	4	5
5.	Negative attitudes of others towards housewives	1	2	3	4	5
6.	Not living up to my potential in my career	1	2	3	4	5
7.	Feeling lonely	1	2	3	4	5
8.	Feeling bored	1	2	3	4	5
9.	Feeling fatigued	1	2	3	4	5
10.	Not having enough time to myself	1	2	3	4	5
11.	My husband not having enough time to spend with our child as he should	1	2	3	4	5
12.	My husband not living up to his potential in his career	1	2	3	4	5
13.	My husband feeling fatigued	1	2	3	4	5
14.	My husband not having enough time to himself	1	2	3	4	5

ATTITUDES AND BELIEFS

PLEASE INDICATE HOW STRONGLY YOU AGREE OR DISAGREE WITH THE FOLLOWING STATEMENTS

    1 = strongly agree
    2 = moderately agree
    3 = agree slightly more than disagree
    4 = disagree slightly more than agree
    5 = moderately disagree
    6 = strongly disagree

1. Women with children in grammar school should, if at all possible, stay at home rather than work. 1 2 3 4 5

2. I would feel uncomfortable if my immediate supervisor at work was a woman. 1 2 3 4 5

3. Since men have a natural urge to dominate and lead, women who challenge this actually threaten the welfare of society. 1 2 3 4 5

4. Taking care of children is important work. 1 2 3 4 5

5. In general, the married, professional woman is able to adequately meet her responsibilities to both her family and career. 1 2 3 4 5

6. A man's self-esteem is severely injured if his wife makes more money than he does. 1 2 3 4 5

7. There should be low-cost, high quality childcare centers for working women. 1 2 3 4 5

8. Children with full-time mothers turn out better. 1 2 3 4 5

9. Men should have more freedom to do such things as cook and care for children, if they so desire. 1 2 3 4 5

10. In general, the full-time homemaker fulfills her obligations to her family better than the married, professional woman who is employed full-time. 1 2 3 4 5

11. There is considerable evidence that men, in general, are a "superior species" to women. 1 2 3 4 5

12. Women with preschool children should not work - if at all possible. 1 2 3 4 5

13. Men should stop appraising women solely on the basis of appearance and sex appeal. 1 2 3 4 5

14. Most people don't respect mothers. 1 2 3 4 5

15. It is possible for women to satisfy their needs for achievement through their husbands. 1 2 3 4 5

16. The needs of children from homes where the mother is employed in a profession are met as well as the needs of children from homes where the mother is a homemaker. 1 2 3 4 5

17. Most people think women lose their sex appeal when they become mothers. 1 2 3 4 5

18. Females should go ahead and pamper males - "Tell him how great he is" - because that is a useful way to get what they want. 1 2 3 4 5

19. To a great extent, women are less able to make a career commitment than men are. 1 2 3 4 5

20. The Equal Rights Amendment related to sex should be ratified as soon as possible. 1 2 3 4 5

21. If the married, professional woman discontinues her employment to assume a full-time homemaking role, it necessarily follows that she will better fulfill her family obligations. 1 2 3 4 5

22. Women should have equal job opportunities with men. 1 2 3 4 5

23. Career women generally are neurotic. 1 2 3 4 5

24. Men's clubs and lodges should be required to admit women. 1 2 3 4 5

INDICATE HOW STRONGLY YOU AGREE OR DISAGREE WITH THE FOLLOWING STATEMENTS
    1 = strongly agree
    2 = moderately agree
    3 = agree slightly more than disagree
    4 = disagree slightly more than agree
    5 = moderately disagree
    6 = strongly disagree

25. Whoever is the better wage-earner, wife or husband, should be the breadwinner. 1 2 3 4 5 6

26. Most people think mothers are uninteresting. 1 2 3 4 5 6

27. Women should be encouraged to plan for a career, not just a job. 1 2 3 4 5 6

28. Women are less capable of making important decisions than men are. 1 2 3 4 5 6

29. Some professions of the married, employed woman interfere more than others with her ability to fulfill her family obligations. 1 2 3 4 5 6

30. Either consciously or unconsciously, most women would like to be men. 1 2 3 4 5 6

31. A husband who is the breadwinner in the family should make all the important decisions. 1 2 3 4 5 6

32. I would vote for a woman for President of the United States. 1 2 3 4 5 6

33. People assume mothers are too involved with their children. 1 2 3 4 5 6

34. Women really like being dependent on men. 1 2 3 4 5 6

35. Men need liberation equally as much as women do. 1 2 3 4 5 6

36. In general, the professional, married woman chooses to work to satisfy personal rather than economic needs. 1 2 3 4 5 6

37. Women can attain true equality in this country only through a really drastic change in the social structure. 1 2 3 4 5 6

38. Women generally prefer light conversations over rational discussions. 1 2 3 4 5 6

39. Women should get equal pay with men for doing the same jobs. 1 2 3 4 5 6

40. The way men and women behave is more a result of their genetic makeup than of the way they were brought up. 1 2 3 4 5 6

41. Women are as capable as men of enjoying a full sex life. 1 2 3 4 5 6

42. Men should take the same amount of responsibility as women in caring for home and children. 1 2 3 4 5 6

43. Men are more capable of assuming leadership than women are. 1 2 3 4 5 6

COMMENTS

If you felt there were any areas in which the questionnaire did not allow
sufficient room to respond fully, or which you felt should have been
covered but were not, please feel free to use the space below to explain
in more detail.

A follow-up study is now being planned. This study would focus on the carrying out of plans to either continue or interrupt one's career as well as look at changes in plans that occurred after the baby is born. Would you be willing to take part in this study?

If so, would you be willing to complete another mailed questionnaire in the future? ____ Yes ____ No

Would you be willing to be interviewed? ____ Yes ____ No
If you answered yes to either or both questions, please print your name, address and phone number below. Thank you.

Name _____

Address _____

_____

Phone _____

Would you like a copy of the results of this study? ____ Yes ____ No
If so, and you have not written your name and address above, please do so below.

Name _____

Address _____

_____

YOU HAVE NOW COMPLETED THE QUESTIONNAIRE. PLEASE REMEMBER TO RETURN IT TO ME AT YOUR NEXT CLASS MEETING. THANK YOU VERY MUCH.

Husband's Questionnaire

Dear Participant,

Thank you for agreeing to participate in this study of women and their husbands who are having their first child. As explained, the study is an attempt to investigate what factors influence women like your wife to plan to either continue or interrupt their careers after their child is born. As a husband and a future father, your thoughts and concerns about this decision are a valuable source of information that can contribute to our understanding of some of the issues and concerns that many couples in our society face today.

The attached questionnaire asks about future plans, your beliefs about the role of women and men in today's society and your personal characteristics. Please be assured that your responses will be kept completely confidential. While each individual is very important, findings will report overall patterns of response and not single out individuals.

I hope that you will find time to complete the questionnaire in the next week and return it to me at your next class meeting. Full and complete responses from all those who agreed to participate is important for the accuracy of this study. If you have any questions at all, please feel free to call me at 743-6705 (evenings.)

Thank you for your cooperation and your time.

Sincerely,

Debra Behrman
Northwestern University

INSTRUCTIONS

The following questions are of a few basic types. In most cases, <u>and unless otherwise indicated</u>, you are asked to circle the number of the response that best applies for you. For other questions, a brief written response is required. A third type asks you to rank order a set of statements.

While the questionnaire may seem rather long, most of it requires only brief answers and goes very quickly. Your responses will be kept strictly confidential.

Please answer all items as frankly as possible. We are interested in what <u>you</u> think; please don't ask others for their opinions.

Thank you.

Date _____

BACKGROUND INFORMATION

1. YOUR AGE _____   2. WIFE'S AGE _____

3. WHAT IS YOUR MARITAL STATUS?

      1. Married   4. Divorced
      2. Remarried   5. Widowed
      3. Separated

4. HOW LONG HAVE YOU BEEN MARRIED? _____

5. WHAT IS YOUR RACE?

      1. Caucasian   3. Hispanic
      2. Black   4. Other (please specify) _____

6. WHAT IS YOUR RELIGION?

      1. Protestant   4. None
      2. Catholic   5. Other (please specify) _____
      3. Jewish

7. WHAT IS YOUR LEVEL OF EDUCATION?

      a. Highest grade completed (please circle)

           High School   College   Graduate School
           9 10 11 12   1 2 3 4   1 2 3 4 5 6

      b. Degrees obtained; specialized training received, etc.

      _____

8. WHAT IS YOUR PRESENT OCCUPATION? (please be specific)

9. JUST PRIOR TO YOUR WIFE'S PREGNANCY, WERE YOU

      1. Working full-time   Hours per week? _____
      2. Working part-time   Hours per week? _____
      3. Student   Full-time ____ Part-time ____ Degree sought ___
      4. Not employed but looking for work
      5. Not employed
      6. Other (please explain) _____

10. NUMBER OF YEARS AT YOUR OCCUPATION _____

11. IF YOUR EMPLOYMENT STATUS HAS CHANGED SINCE YOUR WIFE'S PREGNANCY, PLEASE EXPLAIN

12. YOUR INCOME (not including wife's) _____

13. DOES YOUR EMPLOYER HAVE ANY POLICY REGARDING PATERNITY LEAVE?

14. HOW FLEXIBLE IS YOUR CURRENT JOB IN TERMS OF WORK SCHEDULE?

very		somewhat		not at all
1	2	3	4	5

15. HOW FLEXIBLE IS YOUR WIFE'S CURRENT JOB (OR LAST HELD JOB) IN TERMS OF WORK SCHEDULE?

very		somewhat		not at all
1	2	3	4	5

16. WHAT IS YOUR CHILD'S EXPECTED BIRTHDATE? _____

17. THE PREGNANCY WAS

    1. planned
    2. unplanned

18. HOW MANY CHILDREN WOULD YOU LIKE TO HAVE? _____

FUTURE PLANS

1. AFTER THE BIRTH OF YOUR BABY, WHAT ARE YOUR WIFE'S PLANS REGARDING EMPLOYMENT?

    1. Return to work full-time
    2. Return to work part-time   Hours per week? _____
    3. Attend school   full-time _____ part-time _____
    4. No plans to return to work during the first year
    5. She has not decided yet, but will do so before baby is born
    6. She has not decided yet; will wait to see what happens after baby is born
    7. Other (please explain) _____

2. HOW DEFINITE ARE HER PLANS?

    1. Very definite; all arrangements have been made
    2. Pretty definite
    3. Somewhat definite; details need to be worked out
    4. Not very definite
    5. Not at all definite; she really hasn't made any final arrangements

3. HOW CERTAIN DO YOU FEEL THAT SHE WILL ACTUALLY CARRY OUT THESE PLANS?

    1. Very certain that this is what she will do
    2. Pretty certain
    3. Fairly certain but she may change her plans
    4. Not very certain
    5. Not at all certain; I really think she will change her plans later

4. AFTER THE BIRTH OF YOUR BABY, WHAT ARE YOUR PLANS REGARDING EMPLOYMENT?

    1. Work full-time   Hours per week? _____
    2. Work part-time   Hours per week? _____
    3. Attend school   Full-time ___ Part-time ___ Degree sought? _____
    4. No plans to return to work during the first year
    5. I have not decided yet; will do so before baby is born
    6. I have not decided yet; will wait to see what happens after baby is born
    7. Other (please explain) _____

5. IF YOU PLAN TO CHANGE YOUR EMPLOYMENT STATUS AFTER THE BIRTH OF YOUR BABY, PLEASE EXPLAIN, GIVING YOUR REASONS.

RELATED FACTORS

1. HOW EASY OR DIFFICULT HAS IT BEEN FOR YOU AND YOUR WIFE TO DECIDE WHAT TO DO REGARDING EMPLOYMENT AFTER THE BIRTH OF YOUR BABY?

    1. Very easy; we knew exactly what we were going to do
    2. Pretty easy
    3. Neither easy nor difficult; we had an idea about what we were going to do but were not completely certain
    4. Pretty difficult
    5. Very difficult; we experienced a lot of conflict in making this decision

2. HOW COMFORTABLE OR UNCOMFORTABLE DO YOU FEEL ABOUT YOUR WIFE'S PLANS TO EITHER RETURN TO WORK OR REMAIN HOME WITH YOUR CHILD?

    1. Very comfortable
    2. Pretty comfortable
    3. Both comfortable and uncomfortable; there's no perfect plan
    4. Pretty uncomfortable
    5. Very uncomfortable

3. WHOSE DECISION IS IT, YOURS OR YOUR WIFE'S?

    1. My wife's decision totally
    2. More my wife's decision than mine
    3. Joint decision
    4. More my decision than my wife's

4. HOW MUCH HAVE YOU AND YOUR WIFE DISCUSSED THIS ISSUE?

a great deal		some		not at all
1	2	3	4	5

5. WAS THERE ANY DISAGREEMENT BETWEEN YOU ABOUT THIS ISSUE?

a great deal		some		none at all
1	2	3	4	5

6. WHAT WOULD YOU PREFER YOUR WIFE DO WITHIN THE NEXT YEAR AFTER YOUR BABY IS BORN?

1. Return to work full-time
2. Return to work part-time
3. Not work outside the home
4. No preference
5. Other (Please explain) _____

7. WHAT WOULD YOU PREFER TO DO AFTER YOUR BABY IS BORN?

1. Work full-time
2. Work part-time
3. Not work outside the home
4. Other (Please explain) _____

8. DID YOU DISCUSS THIS ISSUE WITH ANY OF THE FOLLOWING?
   (Please circle all that apply)

1. Parents
2. Other family members
3. Friends
4. Colleagues
5. Professional consultants (clergy, psychologists, educators, etc.)
6. Other (please specify) _____

9. HOW MUCH INFLUENCE DID EACH OF THE FOLLOWING HAVE ON THIS DECISION?

	None		Some		A great deal
1. Parents	1	2	3	4	5
2. Other family members	1	2	3	4	5
3. Friends	1	2	3	4	5
4. Colleagues	1	2	3	4	5
5. Professional consultants	1	2	3	4	5
6. Other	1	2	3	4	5

10. PLEASE RANK IN ORDER OF IMPORTANCE (NUMBER 1 BEING MOST IMPORTANT) WHICHEVER
    OF THE FOLLOWING ARE THE MAJOR REASONS FOR YOUR WIFE'S PLANS

_____ Financial considerations
_____ Needs of our child
_____ Practical considerations (e.g. child-care, flexibility of hours, etc.)
_____ My wife's needs and desires
_____ Career considerations
_____ My needs and desires
_____ Available job opportunities

11. HOW IMPORTANT ARE EACH OF THESE FACTORS IN THIS DECISION?

		Very imp't		Somewhat imp't		Not imp
1.	Financial considerations	1	2	3	4	5
2.	Needs of our child	1	2	3	4	5
3.	Practical considerations	1	2	3	4	5
4.	My wife's needs and desires	1	2	3	4	5
5.	Career considerations	1	2	3	4	5
6.	My needs and desires	1	2	3	4	5
7.	Available job opportunities	1	2	3	4	5

12. IF THERE ARE OTHER FACTORS THAT WERE INVOLVED IN THIS DECISION THAT ARE NOT INCLUDED IN THE ABOVE, PLEASE DESCRIBE BELOW.

13. WHAT DO YOU THINK YOUR WIFE WOULD <u>IDEALLY</u> PREFER TO DO REGARDING EMPLOYMENT DURING YOUR CHILD'S FIRST YEAR?

    1. Return to work full-time
    2. Return to work part-time
    3. Not work outside the home at all
    4. Attend school
    5. Other (Please explain) _____

14. EVERYONE HAS A VARIETY OF DIFFERENT ROLES IN LIFE (e.g. SPOUSE, WORKER, FRIEND, etc.) THESE CAN BE DIVIDED INTO ROUGHLY THREE MAJOR AREAS: CAREER OR WORK ROLES, HOME AND FAMILY ROLES AND PERSONAL ROLES. HOW IMPORTANT ARE EACH OF THESE TO YOUR PERSONAL IDENTITY?

		Very imp't		Somewhat imp't		Not imp't
1.	Career or work roles	1	2	3	4	5
2.	Home and family roles	1	2	3	4	5
3.	Personal roles	1	2	3	4	5

15. PLEASE RANK THE IMPORTANCE OF THESE ROLES TO YOU WITH NUMBER 1 BEING MOST IMPORTANT

    _____ Career or work roles
    _____ Home and family roles
    _____ Personal roles

16. HOW IMPORTANT DO YOU THINK YOUR WIFE'S ROLES ARE TO HER?

		Very imp't		Somewhat imp't		Not imp't
1.	Career or work roles	1	2	3	4	5
2.	Home and family roles	1	2	3	4	5
3.	Personal roles	1	2	3	4	5

17. PLEASE RANK THESE ROLES IN TERMS OF THE IMPORTANCE YOU THINK THEY HAVE TO YOUR WIFE (WITH NUMBER 1 BEING MOST IMPORTANT)

    _____ Career or work roles
    _____ Home and family roles
    _____ Personal roles

18. HOW DO YOU FEEL ABOUT YOUR WIFE'S CAREER?

    1. Very positive; I very much like the idea of her having a career
    2. Somewhat positive
    3. Neutral; I don't care one way or the other
    4. Somewhat negative
    5. Very negative; I would much prefer that she not have a career at all

19. HOW SUPPORTIVE DO YOU THINK YOU HAVE BEEN OF YOUR WIFE'S CAREER PURSUITS UP TO NOW?

    1. Unconditional and active support
    2. Unconditional but inactive support
    3. Conditional support
    4. Resigned to it
    5. Have actively discouraged it

20. OVERALL, HOW SATISFIED OR DISSATISFIED HAVE YOU BEEN WITH YOUR CAREER TO DATE?

Very satisfied		Neutral		Very dissatisfied
1	2	3	4	5

21. OVERALL, HOW SATISFIED OR DISSATISFIED HAVE YOU BEEN WITH YOUR MARRIAGE TO DATE?

Very satisfied		Neutral		Very dissatisfied
1	2	3	4	5

22. OVERALL, HOW SATISFIED OR DISSATISFIED DO YOU THINK YOUR WIFE HAS BEEN WITH HER CAREER TO DATE?

Very satisfied		Neutral		Very dissatisfied
1	2	3	4	5

23. OVERALL, HOW SATISFIED OR DISSATISFIED DO YOU THINK YOUR WIFE HAS BEEN WITH YOUR MARRIAGE TO DATE?

Very satisfied		Neutral		Very dissatisfied
1	2	3	4	5

24. HERE IS A LIST OF THINGS A PERSON COULD HAVE ON HIS JOB. HOW IMPORTANT HAVE EACH OF THE FOLLOWING BEEN TO YOU ON YOUR JOB?

	Not very Important		Moderately Important			Extremely Important	
1. The amount of pay you get	1	2	3	4	5	6	7
2. The quality of the equipment you work with	1	2	3	4	5	6	7
3. Your chances of getting a promotion	1	2	3	4	5	6	7
4. The physical surroundings on your job	1	2	3	4	5	6	7
5. The chances you have to accomplish something worthwhile	1	2	3	4	5	6	7
6. The chances you have to learn new things	1	2	3	4	5	6	7
7. The chances you have to do something that makes you feel good about yourself as a person	1	2	3	4	5	6	7
8. The chances you have to do the things that you do best	1	2	3	4	5	6	7
9. The chances you have to do a variety of different things	1	2	3	4	5	6	7
10. The friendliness of the people you work with	1	2	3	4	5	6	7
11. The way your supervisor treats you	1	2	3	4	5	6	7
12. The respect you receive from the people you work with	1	2	3	4	5	6	7
13. Your fringe benefits	1	2	3	4	5	6	7
14. The opportunity to think about other things besides your work	1	2	3	4	5	6	7
15. The opportunity to develop your skills and abilities	1	2	3	4	5	6	7
16. The freedom to talk with people on the job	1	2	3	4	5	6	7
17. The chances you have to move around during your working day	1	2	3	4	5	6	7

25. WHO DO YOU THINK SHOULD BE RESPONSIBLE FOR PROVIDING FOR A FAMILY FINANCIALLY?

    1. Mainly wife
    2. Wife more than husband
    3. Wife and husband equally
    4. Husband more than wife
    5. Mainly husband

26. WHO DO YOU THINK SHOULD BE RESPONSIBLE FOR HOUSEHOLD TASKS?

    1. Mainly wife
    2. Wife more than husband
    3. Wife and husband equally
    4. Husband more than wife
    5. Mainly husband

27. WHO PERFORMS HOUSEHOLD TASKS NOW?

    1. Mainly wife
    2. Wife more than husband
    3. Wife and husband equally
    4. Husband more than wife
    5. Mainly husband

28. WHO DO YOU THINK SHOULD BE RESPONSIBLE FOR CARE OF AN INFANT?

    1. Mainly wife
    2. Wife more than husband
    3. Wife and husband equally
    4. Husband more than wife
    5. Mainly husband

29. AFTER YOUR BABY IS BORN, WHO DO YOU THINK WILL BE RESPONSIBLE FOR HIS OR HER CARE?

    1. Mainly wife
    2. Wife more than husband
    3. Wife and husband equally
    4. Husband more than wife
    5. Mainly husband

30. AFTER YOUR BABY IS BORN, WHO DO YOU THINK WILL PERFORM HOUSEHOLD TASKS?

    1. Mainly wife
    2. Wife more than husband
    3. Wife and husband equally
    4. Husband more than wife
    5. Mainly husband

31. IN YOUR OPINION, FOR A MOTHER TO BE EMPLOYED BY CHOICE (NOT DUE TO FINANCIAL NECESSITY) HER ONLY OR YOUNGEST CHILD SHOULD BE AT LEAST

    1. Six months or less
    2. Six months to a year
    3. One to two years
    4. Two to three years
    5. Three to five years
    6. School-age or older

32. GIVE YOUR ESTIMATE OF WHAT YOUR WIFE WOULD SAY TO THE ABOVE QUESTION

    1. Six months or less
    2. Six months to a year
    3. One to two years
    4. Two to three years
    5. Three to five years
    6. School-age or older

33. GIVE YOUR ESTIMATE OF WHAT YOUR MOTHER WOULD SAY TO THE ABOVE QUESTION

    1. Six months or less
    2. Six months to a year
    3. One to two years
    4. Two to three years
    5. Three to five years
    6. School-age or older

34. THE PREVAILING SOCIAL VIEW IN THE U.S. WOULD SAY THAT THE AGE OF THE CHILD IN THE ABOVE CASE SHOULD BE:

    1. Six months or less
    2. Six months to a year
    3. One to two years
    4. Two to three years
    5. Three to five years
    6. School-age or older

35. HOW BOTHERED WOULD YOU BE IF ANY OF THE FOLLOWING OCCURRED DURING THE NEXT YEAR?

		Very		Somewhat		Not at all
1.	Not having enough time to spend with my child as I would like	1	2	3	4	5
2.	My not having enough time together with my wife as I would like	1	2	3	4	5
3.	My wife not having enough time to spend with our child as she should	1	2	3	4	5
4.	Not having enough time to devote to my career as I would like	1	2	3	4	5
5.	Negative attitudes of others towards working mothers	1	2	3	4	5
6.	Negative attitudes of others towards housewives	1	2	3	4	5
7.	My wife not living up to her potential in her career	1	2	3	4	5
8.	My not living up to my potential in my career	1	2	3	4	5
9.	My wife feeling lonely	1	2	3	4	5
10.	My wife feeling bored	1	2	3	4	5
11.	My wife feeling fatigued	1	2	3	4	5
12.	My wife not having enough time to herself	1	2	3	4	5
13.	My feeling fatigued	1	2	3	4	5
14.	My not having enough time to myself	1	2	3	4	5

ATTITUDES AND BELIEFS

PLEASE INDICATE HOW STRONGLY YOU AGREE OR DISAGREE WITH THE FOLLOWING STATEMENTS

        1 = strongly agree
        2 = moderately agree
        3 = agree slightly more than disagree
        4 = disagree slightly more than agree
        5 = moderately disagree
        6 = strongly disagree

1. Women with children in grammar school should, if at all possible, stay at home rather than work.   1 2 3 4 5 6

2. I would feel uncomfortable if my immediate supervisor at work was a woman.   1 2 3 4 5 6

3. Since men have a natural urge to dominate and lead, women who challenge this actually threaten the welfare of society.   1 2 3 4 5 6

4. Taking care of children is important work.   1 2 3 4 5 6

5. In general, the married, professional woman is able to adequately meet her responsibilities to both her family and career.   1 2 3 4 5 6

6. A man's self-esteem is severely injured if his wife makes more money than he does.   1 2 3 4 5 6

7. There should be low-cost, high quality childcare centers for working women.   1 2 3 4 5 6

8. Children with full-time mothers turn out better.   1 2 3 4 5 6

9. Men should have more freedom to do such things as cook and care for children, if they so desire.   1 2 3 4 5 6

10. In general, the full-time homemaker fulfills her obligations to her family better than the married, professional woman who is employed full-time.   1 2 3 4 5 6

11. There is considerable evidence that men, in general, are a "superior species" to women.   1 2 3 4 5 6

12. Women with preschool children should not work - if at all possible.   1 2 3 4 5 6

13. Men should stop appraising women solely on the basis of appearance and sex appeal.   1 2 3 4 5 6

14. Most people don't respect mothers.   1 2 3 4 5 6

15. It is possible for women to satisfy their needs for achievement through their husbands.   1 2 3 4 5 6

16. The needs of children from homes where the mother is employed in a profession are met as well as the needs of children from homes where the mother is a homemaker.   1 2 3 4 5 6

17. Most people think women lose their sex appeal when they become mothers.   1 2 3 4 5 6

18. Females should go ahead and pamper males - "Tell him how great he is" - because that is a useful way to get what they want.   1 2 3 4 5 6

19. To a great extent, women are less able to make a career commitment than men are.   1 2 3 4 5 6

20. The Equal Rights Amendment related to sex should be ratified as soon as possible.   1 2 3 4 5 6

21. If the married, professional woman discontinues her employment to assume a full-time homemaking role, it necessarily follows that she will better fulfill her family obligations.   1 2 3 4 5 6

22. Women should have equal job opportunities with men.   1 2 3 4 5 6

23. Career women generally are neurotic.   1 2 3 4 5 6

24. Men's clubs and lodges should be required to admit women.   1 2 3 4 5 6

25. Whoever is the better wage-earner, wife or husband, should be the breadwinner.   1 2 3 4 5 6

INDICATE HOW STRONGLY YOU AGREE OR DISAGREE WITH THE FOLLOWING STATEMENTS
- 1 = strongly agree
- 2 = moderately agree
- 3 = agree slightly more than disagree
- 4 = disagree slightly more than agree
- 5 = moderately disagree
- 6 = strongly disagree

26. Most people think mothers are uninteresting.   1 2 3 4 5 6

27. Women should be encouraged to plan for a career, not just a job.   1 2 3 4 5 6

28. Women are less capable of making important decisions than men are.   1 2 3 4 5 6

29. Some professions of the married, employed woman interfere more than others with her ability to fulfill her family obligations.   1 2 3 4 5 6

30. Either consciously or unconsciously, most women would like to be men.   1 2 3 4 5 6

31. A husband who is the breadwinner in the family should make all the important decisions.   1 2 3 4 5 6

32. I would vote for a woman for President of the United States.   1 2 3 4 5 6

33. People assume mothers are too involved with their children.   1 2 3 4 5 6

34. Women really like being dependent on men.   1 2 3 4 5 6

35. Men need liberation equally as much as women do.   1 2 3 4 5 6

36. In general, the professional, married woman chooses to work to satisfy personal rather than economic needs.   1 2 3 4 5 6

37. Women can attain true equality in this country only through a really drastic change in the social structure.   1 2 3 4 5 6

38. Women generally prefer light conversations over rational discussions.   1 2 3 4 5 6

39. Women should get equal pay with men for doing the same jobs.   1 2 3 4 5 6

40. The way men and women behave is more a result of their genetic makeup than of the way they were brought up.   1 2 3 4 5 6

41. Women are as capable as men of enjoying a full sex life.   1 2 3 4 5 6

42. Men should take the same amount of responsibility as women in caring for home and children.   1 2 3 4 5 6

43. Men are more capable of assuming leadership than women are.   1 2 3 4 5 6

COMMENTS

If you felt there were any areas in which the questionnaire did not allow sufficient room to respond fully, or which you felt should have been covered but were not, please feel free to use the space below to explain in more detail.

A follow-up study is now being planned. This study would focus on the carrying out of plans to either continue or interrupt one's career as well as look at changes in plans that occurred after the baby is born. Would you be willing to take part in this study?

If so, would you be willing to complete another mailed questionnaire in the future? _____ Yes _____ No

Would you be willing to be interviewed? _____ Yes _____ No
If you answered yes to either or both questions, please print your name, address and phone number below. Thank you.

    Name   _____
    Address   _____
              _____
    Phone   _____

Would you like a copy of the results of this study? _____ Yes _____ No
If so, and you have not written your name and address above, please do so below.

    Name   _____
    Address   _____
              _____

YOU HAVE NOW COMPLETED THE QUESTIONNAIRE. PLEASE REMEMBER TO RETURN IT TO ME AT YOUR NEXT CLASS MEETING. THANK YOU VERY MUCH.

Bibliography

Aldous, J. The making of family roles and family change. *The Family Coordinator*, 1974, *23*, 231–35.

Almquist, E. M. Attitudes of college men toward working wives. *The Vocational Guidance Quarterly*, 1974, *23*, 115–21.

_____. Women in the labor force. *Signs: Journal of Women in Culture and Society*, 1977, *2*, 843–55.

Almquist, E. M., and Angrist, S. Career salience and atypicality of occupational choice among college women. *Journal of Marriage and the Family*, 1970, *32*, 242–49.

Altman, S., and Grossman, F. K. Women's career plans and maternal employment. *Psychology of Women Quarterly*, 1977, *1*, 365–76.

Angrist, S. S. Role conception as a predictor of adult female roles. *Sociology and Social Research*, 1966, *50*, 448–59.

_____. Variations in women's adult aspirations during college. *Journal of Marriage and the Family*, 1972, *34*, 465–68.

Angrist, S. S., Lave, J. R., and Mickelsen, R. How working mothers manage: Socioeconomic differences in work, child care and household tasks. *Social Science Quarterly*, 1976, *56*, 631–37.

Applegarth, A. Some observations on work inhibitions in women. In H. P. Blum, ed., *Female Psychology: Contemporary Psychoanalytic Views*, New York: International Universities Press, Inc., 1977.

Araji, S. K. Husbands' and wives' attitude behavior congruence on family roles. *Journal of Marriage and the Family*, 1977, *39*, 309–20.

Arnott, C. Husbands' attitude and wives' commitment to employment. *Journal of Marriage and the Family*, 1972, *34*, 673–84.

Astin, A. W., and Nichols, R. C. Life goals and vocational choice. *Journal of Applied Psychology*, 1964, *48*, 50–58.

Astle, D. J. U.S. men and women's attitudes toward female sex roles. (Doctoral dissertation, Oklahoma State University, 1978). *Dissertation Abstracts International*, 1979, *39*, 5152. (University Microfilms No. 7903640).

Bailyn, L. Notes on the role of choice in the psychology of professional women. *Daedalus*, 1964, *93*, 700–709.

_____. Career and family orientations of husbands and wives in relation to marital happiness. *Human Relations*, 1970, *23*, 97–113.

Bardwick, J., and Douvan, E. The socialization of women. In V. Gornick and B. K. Moran, eds., *Women in Sexist Society: Studies in Power and Powerlessness*. New York: Basic Books, 1971.

Barnett, R. Personality correlates of vocational planning. *Genetic Psychology Monographs*, 1971, *83*, 309–56.

Baruch, G. K. Maternal influences upon college women's attitudes toward women and work. *Developmental Psychology,* 1972, *6,* 32–37.

———. Feminine self-esteem, self-ratings of competence, and maternal career commitment. *Journal of Counseling Psychology,* 1973, *20,* 487–88.

———. Maternal career-orientation as related to paternal identification in college women. *Journal of Vocational Behavior,* 1974, *4,* 173–80.

Baruch, R. The achievement motive in women: implications for career development. *Journal of Personality and Social Psychology,* 1967, *5,* 260–67.

Bayer, A. E. Sexist students in American colleges: A descriptive note. *Journal of Marriage and the Family,* 1975, *37,* 391–97.

Bebbington, A. C. The function of stress in the establishment of the dual-career family. *Journal of Marriage and the Family,* 1973, *35,* 530–37.

Bell, C. Occupational career, family cycle and extended family relations. *Human Relations,* 1971, *24,* 463–75.

Bem, S. L., and Bem, D. J. We're all nonconscious sexists. *Psychology Today,* November 1970, pp. 22–26; 115–16.

Bernard, J. *The Future of Marriage.* New York: World Publishing, 1972.

Bettelheim, B. The commitment required of a woman entering a scientific profession in present-day American society. In J. A. Mattfield and C. G. Van Aken, eds., *Women and the Scientific Professions.* Cambridge, Massachusetts: M.I.T. Press, 1965.

Bielby, D.D.V. Maternal employment and socioeconomic status as factors in daughters' career salience: some substantive refinements. *Sex Roles.* 1978, *4,* 249–65.

Birnbaum, J. A. Life patterns, personality style and self esteem in gifted family oriented and career committed women. (Doctoral dissertation, The University of Michigan, 1971). *Dissertation Abstracts International,* 1971, *32,* 1834B. (University Microfilms No. 71-23, 698).

———. Life patterns and self-esteem in gifted family-oriented and career-committed women. In M. Mednick, S. Tangri and L. Hoffman, eds., *Women and Achievement.* Washington, D. C.: Hemisphere Publishing Corporation, 1975.

Blitz, R. C. Women in the professions. *Monthly Labor Review,* 1974, *97*(5), 34–40.

Bowlby, J. *Attachment and Loss,* Vol. 1. London: The Hogarth Press and the Institute of Psychoanalysis, 1969.

Brazelton, T. B. *Infants and Mothers.* New York: Dell Publishing Co., 1969.

Breedlove, C. J., and Cicirelli, V. G. Women's fear of success in relation to personal characteristics and type of occupation. *The Journal of Psychology,* 1974, *86,* 181–190.

Brizard, R. H. Two days in one: Portraits of professional women with families in France and America. (Doctoral dissertation, The Wright Institute, 1977). *Dissertation Abstracts International,* 1978, *38,* 3866-3867B. (University Microfilms No. 7730344).

Brogan, D., and Kutner, N. Measuring sex-role orientation: A normative approach. *Journal of Marriage and the Family,* 1976, *38,* 31–39.

Broverman, I., Vogel, S., Broverman, D., Clarkson, F. and Rosenkrantz, P. Sex-role stereotypes: A current appraisal. *The Journal of Social Issues,* 1972, *28*(2), 59–78.

Burke, R., and Weir, T. Some personality differences between members of one-career and two-career families. *Journal of Marriage and the Family,* 1976, *38,* 453–60.

Carmichael, C. A. More women choosing both families and careers. *Chicago Tribune,* March 23, 1980.

Cartwright, L. K. Continuity and noncontinuity in the careers of a sample of young women physicians. *Journal of the American Medical Women's Association,* 1977, *32,* 316–21.

———. Career satisfaction and role harmony in a sample of young women physicians. *Journal of Vocational Behavior,* 1978, *12,* 184–96.

Chafe, W. H. *Women and Equality: Changing Patterns in American Culture.* New York: Oxford University Press, 1977.

Clavan, S. Women's liberation and the family. *The Family Coordinator,* 1970, *19,* 317–23.

Coser, R., and Rokoff, G. Women in the occupational world: Social disruption and conflict. *Social Problems,* 1970, *18,* 535–54.

Cummings, L. D. Value stretch in definitions of career among college women: Horatia Alger as feminist model. *Social Problems,* 1977, *25,* 65–74.

Darley, S. A. Big-time careers for the little women: A dual-role dilemma. *Journal of Social Issues,* 1976, *32*(3), 85–98.

Davis, F., and Olesen, V. L. The career outlook of professionally educated women. *Psychiatry,* 1965, *28,* 334–45.

Devine, R., and Stillion, J. An examination of locus of control and sex role orientation. *The Journal of Psychology,* 1978, *98,* 75–79.

DiSabatino, M. Psychological factors inhibiting women's occupational aspirations and vocational choices: Implications for counseling. *Vocational Guidance Quarterly,* 1976, *25,* 43–49.

Dohrenwend, B. P., and Dohrenwend, B. S. Social and cultural influences on psychopathology. *Annual Review of Psychology,* 1974, *25,* 417–52.

Edwards, C. N. Cultural values and role decisions: A study of educated women. *Journal of Counseling Psychology,* 1969, *16,* 36–40.

Engelhard, P. A., and Jones, K. O. Trends in counselor attitude about women's roles. *Journal of Counseling Psychology,* 1976, *23,* 365–72.

Epstein, C. F. *Women's Place: Options and Limits in Professional Careers.* Berkeley: University of California Press, 1970.

Epstein, G., and Bronzaft, A. Female freshmen view their roles as women. *Journal of Marriage and the Family,* 1972, *34,* 671–72.

Erskine, H. The polls: Women's role. *Public Opinion Quarterly,* 1971, *35,* 275–90.

Etaugh, C. F. Attitudes of professionals toward the married professional woman. *Psychological Reports,* 1973, *32,* 775–80.

Eustace, T. D. Cognitive, attitudinal and socioeconomic factors influencing parents' choice of childbirth procedure (Doctoral dissertation, Fordham University, 1978). *Dissertation Abstracts International,* 1978, *39,* 1474B. (University Microfilms No. 7814888).

Eyde, L. Work motivation of women college graduates: Five year follow-up. *Journal of Counseling Psychology,* 1968, 15, 199–202.

Farley, J. Graduate women: Career aspirations and desired family size. *American Psychologist,* 1970, *25,* 1099–1100.

Farmer, H. S. Helping women resolve the home-career conflict. *Personnel and Guidance Journal,* 1971, *49,* 795–801.

Farmer, H. S., and Bohn, M. J., Jr. Home-career conflict reduction and the level of career interest in women. *Journal of Counseling Psychology,* 1970, *17,* 228–32.

Flapan, M. A paradigm for the analysis of childbearing motivations of married women prior to birth of the first child. *American Journal of Orthopsychiatry,* 1969, *39,* 402–17.

Flapan, M., and Schoenfeld, H. Procedures for exploring women's childbearing motivations, alleviating childbearing conflicts and enhancing maternal role development. *American Journal of Orthopsychiatry,* 1972, *42,* 389–97.

Frankel, P. M. Sex-role attitudes and the development of achievement need in women. *Journal of College Student Personnel,* 1974, *15,* 114–19.

Franks, V., and Burtle, V., eds. *Women in Therapy.* New York: Bruner/Mazel, Inc., 1974.

Friedan, B. *The Feminine Mystique.* New York: W. W. Norton, 1963.

Friedman, J. S. Determinants of career orientation among American females (Doctoral dissertation, Illinois Institute of Technology, 1975). *Dissertation Abstracts International,* 1976, *36,* 3600B. (University Microfilms No. 75-30, 006).

Fuchs, R. Different meanings of employment for women. *Human Relations,* 1971, *24,* 495–99.

Gannon, M., and Hendrickson, D. H. Career orientation and job satisfaction among working wives. *Journal of Applied Psychology,* 1973, *57,* 339–40.

Garland, N. T. The better half? The male in the dual professional family. In C. Safilios-Rothschild, ed., *Toward a Sociology of Women.* Lexington, Massachusetts: Xerox College Publishing, 1972.

Gass, G. Z. Equitable marriage. *The Family Coordinator,* 1974, *23,* 369–72.

Ginzberg, E. *Life Styles of Educated Women.* New York: Columbia University Press, 1966.
────── . *Educated American Women: Life Styles and Self-Portraits.* New York: Columbia University Press, 1971.

Glenn, H. Attitudes regarding gainful employment of married women. *Journal of Home Economics,* 1959, *51,* 247–52.

Gold, A. R. Reexamining barriers to women's career development. *American Journal of Orthopsychiatry,* 1978, *48,* 691–702.

Gordon, F., and Hall, D. T. Self-image and stereotypes of femininity: Their relationship to women's role conflicts and coping. *Journal of Applied Psychology,* 1974, *59,* 241–43.

Graef, R., Csikszentmihalyi, M., and Giffin, P. Enjoyment and work satisfaction. Unpublished manuscript, 1978.

Greenbaum, H. Marriage, family and parenthood. *American Journal of Psychiatry,* 1973, *130,* 1262–65.

Greenhaus, J. H. A factorial investigation of career salience. *Journal of Vocational Behavior,* 1973, *3,* 95–98.

Gump, J. P. Sex-role attitudes and psychological well-being. *The Journal of Social Issues,* 1972, *28*(2), 79–92.

Gysbers, N. C., Johnston, J. A., and Gust, T. Characteristics of homemaker and career-oriented women. *Journal of Counseling Psychology,* 1968, *15,* 541–46.

Hall, D. T. Pressures from work, self and home in the life stages of married women. *Journal of Vocational Behavior,* 1975, *6,* 121–32.

Hall, D. T., and Gordon, F. Career choices of married women: Effects on conflict, role behavior and satisfaction. *Journal of Applied Psychology,* 1973, *58,* 42–48.

Hall, F., and Hall, D. *The two-career couple.* Reading, Massachusetts: Addison-Wesley Publishing Company, 1979.

Haller, M., and Rosenmayr, L. The pluridimensionality of work commitment. *Human Relations,* 1971, *24,* 501–18.

Harmon, L. W. Anatomy of career commitment in women. *Journal of Counseling Psychology.* 1970, *17,* 77–80.

Harrell, J., and Ridley, C. Substitute child care, maternal employment and the quality of mother-child interaction. *Journal of Marriage and the Family,* 1975, *37,* 556–64.

Hawley, M. J. The relationship of women's perceptions of men's views of the feminine ideal to career choice. (Doctoral dissertation, Claremont Graduate School and University Center, 1968). *Dissertation Abstracts International,* 1969, *29,* 2523A. (University Microfilms No. 68-18, 269).

Hawley, P. Perceptions of male models of femininity related to career choice. *Journal of Counseling Psychology,* 1972, *19,* 307–13.

Hayghe, H. Families and the rise of working wives—An overview. *Monthly Labor Review,* 1976, *99*(4), 12–19.

Heckman, N., Bryson, R., and Bryson, J. Problems of professional couples: A content analysis. *Journal of Marriage and the Family,* 1977, *39,* 323–31.

Helson, R. The changing image of the career woman. *The Journal of Social Issues,* 1972, *28*(2), 33–46.

Hennig, M. Family dynamics for developing positive achievement motivation in women: The successful woman executive. *Annals of the New York Academy of Sciences*, 1973, *208*, 76–81.

Herman, J. B., and Gyllstrom, K. K. Working men and women: Inter and intra role conflict. *Psychology of Women Quarterly*, 1977, *1*, 319–33.

Hewer, V., and Neubeck, G. Attitudes of college students toward employment among married women. *Personnel and Guidance Journal*, 1964, *42*, 587–92.

Hilberman, E., Gispert, M., and Harper, J. Impact of a district branch task force on women. *American Journal of Psychiatry*, 1976, *133*, 1159–64.

Hipple, J. L. Perceptual differences between married and single college men for concepts of ideal women. *Adolescence*, 1976, *11*, 579–83.

Hjelle, L. A., and Butterfield, R. Self-actualization and women's attitudes toward their roles in contemporary society. *The Journal of Psychology*, 1974, *87*, 225–30.

Hock, E. Working and nonworking mothers with infants: Perceptions of their careers, their infants' needs, and satisfaction with mothering. *Developmental Psychology*, 1978, *14*, 37–43.

Hoffman, L. W. Early childhood experiences and women's achievement motives. *Journal of Social Issues*, 1972, *28*, 129–56.

Hoffman, L., and Nye, F. I. *Working Mothers.* San Francisco: Jossey-Bass Publishers, 1974.

Holmstrom, L. *The Two-Career Family.* Cambridge, Massachusetts: Schenkman, 1972.

Hopkins, W. P. An analysis of marital adjustment in dual-career and traditional family husbands. (Doctoral dissertation, University of Tennessee, 1976). *Dissertation Abstracts International*, 1977, *37*, 4144–4145B. (University Microfilms No. 77-3646).

Horner, M. S. Toward an understanding of achievement-related conflicts in women. *Journal of Social Issues*, 1972, *28*, 157–76.

Hoyt, D. P., and Kennedy, C. E. Interest and personality correlates of career-motivated and homemaking-motivated college women. *Journal of Counseling Psychology*, 1958, *5*, 44–49.

Huber, J. Sociology. *Signs*, 1976, *1*, 685–97.

Hudis, P. Commitment to work and to family: Marital status differences in women's earnings. *Journal of Marriage and the Family*, 1976, *38*, 267–78.

Humphrey, F. Changing roles for women: Implications for marriage counselors. *Journal of Marriage and the Family*, 1975, *1*, 219–27.

Hunt, J., and Hunt, L. Dilemmas and contradictions of status: The case of the dual career family. *Social Problems*, 1977, *24*, 407–16.

Jackson, D. N. *The Personality Research Form Manual.* Goshen, N.Y.: Research Psychologists Press, 1974.

Johnson, B. Changes in marital and family characteristics of workers: 1970–1978. *Monthly Labor Review*, 1979, *102*(4), 49–52.

————. Marital and family characteristics of the labor force, March 1979. *Monthly Labor Review*, 1980, *103*(4), 48–52.

Johnson, C. L., and Johnson, F. A. Attitudes toward parenting in dual-career families. *American Journal of Psychiatry*, 1977, *134*, 391–95.

Kaley, M. M. Attitudes toward the dual role of the married professional women. *American Psychologist*, 1971, *26*, 301–6.

Keller, S. Does the family have a future? *Journal of Comparative Family Studies*, 1971, *2*, 1–14.

Kerlinger, F. N. *Foundations of Behavioral Research.* Second edition. New York: Holt, Rinehart and Winston, Inc., 1973.

Klecka, W. R. Discriminant analysis. In N. H. Nie, C. H. Hull, J. G. Jenkins, K. Steinbrenner, and D. H. Bent, *Statistical Package for the Social Sciences.* Second edition. New York: McGraw-Hill, 1975.

Komarovsky, M. Cultural contradictions and sex roles. *American Journal of Sociology*, 1946, *52*, 184–89.

————. Cultural contradictions and sex roles: The masculine case. *American Journal of Sociology,* 1973, *78,* 873–84.

Kriger, S. F. nAch and perceived parental child-rearing attitudes of career women and homemakers. *Journal of Vocational Behavior,* 1972, *2,* 419–32.

Lahat-Mandelbaum, B. A woman's decision to work: Demographic, cognitive and personality variables. (Doctoral dissertation, Temple University, 1976). *Dissertation Abstracts International,* 1976, *36,* 6429–6430B. (University Microfilms No. 76-12,014).

Lancaster, J. Coping mechanisms for the working mother. *American Journal of Nursing,* 1975, *75,* 1322–23.

Lefkowitz, M. The women's magazine short-story heroine in 1957 and 1967. In C. Safilios-Rothschild, ed., *Toward a Sociology of Women,* Lexington, Massachusetts: Xerox College Publishing, 1972.

Levine, A. Forging a feminine identity: Women in four professional schools. *The American Journal of Psychoanalysis,* 1975, *35,* 63–67.

Lewin, E., and Damrell, J. Female identity and career pathways. *Sociology of Work and Occupations,* 1978, *5,* 31–34.

Lewis, E. C. *Developing Woman's Potential.* Ames, Iowa: Iowa State University Press, 1968.

Lieberman, M., Reibstein, J., and Sweny, B. Unpublished Manuscript, University of Chicago Research Project, 1979.

Little, K. A question of matrimonial strategy? A comparison of attitudes between Ghanian and British university students. *Journal of Comparative Family Studies,* 1976, *7,* 5–22.

Lopata, H. Z. Social psychological aspects of role involvement. *Sociology and Social Research,* 1969, *53,* 285–98.

Lorber, J. Beyond equality of the sexes: The question of the children. *The Family Coordinator,* 1975, *24,* 465–72.

Maracek, J., and Frasch, C. Locus of control and college women's role expectations. *Journal of Counseling Psychology,* 1977, *24,* 132–36.

Martin, T., Berry, K., and Jacobsen, R. B. The impact of dual-career marriages on female professional careers: An empirical test of a Parsonian hypothesis. *Journal of Marriage and the Family,* 1975, *37,* 734–42.

Masih, L. K. Career saliency and its relation to certain needs, interests and job values. *Personnel and Guidance Journal,* 1967, *45,* 653–58.

Mason, K. O., Czajka, J. L., and Arber, S. Change in U.S. women's sex-role attitudes, 1964–1974. *American Sociological Review,* 1976, *41,* 573–96.

Matthews, E., and Tiedeman, D. V. Attitudes toward career and marriage and the development of life style in young women. *Journal of Counseling Psychology,* 1964, *11,* 375–84.

McArthur, C. Comment on interest and personality correlates of career-motivated and home-making-motivated college women. *Journal of Counseling Psychology,* 1958, *5,* 48–49.

McMillin, M. R. Attitudes of college men toward career involvement of married women. *Vocational Guidance Quarterly,* 1972, *21,* 8–11.

Mead, M. Some theoretical considerations on the problem of mother-child separation. *American Journal of Orthopsychiatry,* 1954, *24,* 471–81.

Mednick, M. S., and Tangri, S. S. New social psychological perspectives on women. *The Journal of Social Issues,* 1972, *28*(2), 1–16.

Mednick, M., Tangri, S., and Hoffman, L., eds. *Women and Achievement.* Washington: Hemisphere Publishing Corporation, 1975.

Meissner, M., Humphreys, E., Meis, S., and Scheu, W. No exit for wives: Sexual division of labour and the cumulation of household demands. *The Canadian Review of Sociology and Anthropology,* 1975, *12,* 424–39.

Miller, T. W. The working mother: Issues and implications for family counselors. *Journal of Family Counseling,* 1976, *4,* 61–65.

Mintz, R. S., and Patterson, C. H. Marriage and career attitudes of women in selected college curriculums. *Vocational Guidance Quarterly,* 1969, *17,* 213–17.

Mulvey, M. C. Psychological and sociological factors in prediction of career patterns of women. *Genetic Psychology Monographs,* 1963, *68.*

Nagely, D. L. Traditional and pioneer working mothers. *Journal of Vocational Behavior,* 1971, *1,* 331–41.

National Opinion Research Center, University of Chicago. *National Data Program for the Social Sciences: Codebook for the Spring 1974 General Social Survey.* Chicago: 1974

Nevill, D., and Damico, S. Development of a role conflict questionnaire for women: Some preliminary findings. *Journal of Consulting and Clinical Psychology,* 1974, *47,* 743.

————. Family size and role conflict in women. *Journal of Psychology,* 1975, *89,* 267–70.

————. Developmental components of role conflict in women. *The Journal of Psychology,* 1977, *95,* 195–98.

Notman, M., and Nadelson, C. Medicine: A career conflict for women. *American Journal of Psychiatry,* 1973, *130,* 1123–27.

Nye, F. I. Sociocultural context. In L. Hoffman and F. I. Nye, eds., *Working Mothers.* San Francisco: Jossey-Bass Publishers, 1974.

————. *Role Structure and Analysis of the Family.* Beverly Hills: Sage Publications, Inc., 1976.

O'Connell, A. N. The relationship between life style and identity synthesis and resynthesis in traditional, neotraditional and nontraditional women. *Journal of Personality,* 1976, *44,* 675–88.

Ohlbaum, J. Self-concepts, value characteristics and self-actualization of professional and non-professional women. (Doctoral dissertation, United States International University, 1971). *Dissertation Abstracts International,* 1971, *32,* 1221B. (University Microfilms No. 71-14, 181).

O'Leary, V. E. Some attitudinal barriers to occupational aspirations in women. *Psychological Bulletin,* 1974, *81,* 809–26.

Oliver, L. W. Achievement and affiliation motivation in career-oriented and homemaking-oriented college women. *Journal of Vocational Behavior,* 1974, *4,* 275–81.

————. The relationship of parental attitudes and parent identification to career and home-making orientation in college women. *Journal of Vocational Behavior,* 1975, *7,* 1–12.

Oliver, W. A. Childbirth expectancies and experiences as a function of locus of control and Lamaze training. (Doctoral dissertation, The Ohio State University, 1972). *Dissertation Abstracts International,* 1973, *33,* 1802-1803B. (University Microfilms No. 72-27, 074).

Oppenheimer, V. K. Demographic influence on female employment and the status of women. *American Journal of Sociology,* 1973, *78,* 946–61.

Orden, S. R., and Bradburn, N. M. Working wives and marriage happiness. *American Journal of Sociology,* 1969, *74,* 392–407.

Osmond, M. W., and Martin, P. Y. Sex and sexism: A comparison of male and female sex-role attitudes. *Journal of Marriage and the Family,* 1975, *37,* 744–58.

Ostrum, A. E. Psychological factors influencing women's choice of childbirth procedure. (Doctoral dissertation, Columbia University, 1972). *Dissertation Abstracts International,* 1973, *33,* 2353B. (University Microfilms No. 72-28, 076).

Otto, H., and Loring, R., eds. *New Life Options.* New York: McGraw Hill Book Company, 1976.

Parelius, A. P. Change and stability in college women's orientations toward education, family and work. *Social Problems,* 1975, *22,* 420–32.

————. Emerging sex-role attitudes, expectations, and strains among college women. *Journal of Marriage and the Family,* 1975, *37,* 146–54.

Parnes, H. S., Shea, J., Spitz, R., and Zeller, F. *Dual careers: A Longitudinal Study of Labor*

Market Experience of Women. Manpower Research Monograph 21. Washington, D. C.: U.S. Government Printing Office, 1970.

Parrish, J. B. Women in professional training. *Monthly Labor Review,* 1974, *97*(5), 40–43.

Parsons, J. E., Frieze, B., and Ruble, D. Intrapsychic factors influencing career aspirations in college women. *Sex Roles,* 1978, *4,* 337–47.

Pearlin, L., and Schooler, C. The structure of coping. *Journal of Health and Social Behavior,* 1978, *19,* 2–22.

Perrucci, C. C. Minority status and the pursuit of professional careers: Women in science and engineering. *Social Forces,* 1970, *49,* 245–59.

Perrucci, C., and Targ, D. Early work orientation and later situational factors as elements of work commitment among married women college graduates. *Sociological Quarterly,* 1978, *19,* 266–80.

Peterson, C., and Peterson, J. Issues concerning collaborating careers. *Journal of Vocational Behavior,* 1975, *7,* 173–80.

Peterson-Hardt, S., and Burlin, F. D. Sex differences in perceptions of familial and occupational roles. *Journal of Vocational Behavior,* 1979, *14,* 306–16.

Pleck, J. H. The male sex role: Definitions, problems and sources of change. *Journal of Social Issues,* 1976, *32,* 155–65.

———. The work-family role system. *Social Problems,* 1977, *24,* 417–27.

Pleck, J. H., Staines, G. L., and Lang, L. Conflicts between work and family life. *Monthly Labor Review,* 1980, *103*(3), 29–31.

Poloma, M. M. Role conflict and the married professional woman. In C. Safilios-Rothschild, ed. *Toward a Sociology of Women.* Lexington, Massachusetts: Xerox College Publishing, 1972.

Poloma, M. M., and Garland, T. N. The married professional woman: A study in the tolerance of domestication. *Journal of Marriage and the Family,* 1971, *33,* 531–39.

Powell, B., and Reznikoff, M. Role conflict and symptoms of psychological distress in college-educated women. *Journal of Consulting and Clinical Psychology,* 1976, *44,* 473–79.

Rand, L. Masculinity or femininity? Differentiating career-oriented and homemaking-oriented college freshman women. *Journal of Counseling Psychology,* 1968, *15,* 444–50.

Rand, L. M., and Miller, A. L. A developmental cross-sectioning of women's careers and marriage attitudes and life plans. *Journal of Vocational Behavior,* 1972, *2,* 317–31.

Rapoport, R., and Rapoport, R. *Dual Career Families Re-examined.* London: Martin Robertson and Co. Ltd., 1976.

———. *Dual Career Families.* Baltimore: Penguin, 1971.

Rapoport, R. and Rapoport, R., eds. *Working Couples.* New York: Harper & Row, 1978.

Rapoport, R., Rapoport, R., and Thiessen, V. Couple symmetry and enjoyment. *Journal of Marriage and the Family,* 1974, *36,* 588–91.

Richardson, M. S. The dimensions of career and work orientation in college women. *Journal of Vocational Behavior,* 1974, *5,* 161–72.

Roby, P. A. Shared parenting: Perspectives from other nations. *School Review,* 1975, *83,* 415–31.

Roper, B., and Labeff, E. Sex roles and feminism revisited: An intergenerational attitude comparison. *Journal of Marriage and the Family,* 1977, *39,* 113–19.

Rose, A. M. The adequacy of women's expectations for adult roles. *Social Forces,* 1951, *30,* 69–77.

Rosen, B., Jerdee, T., and Prestwich, T. Dual-career marital adjustment: Potential effects of dicriminatory managerial attitudes. *Journal of Marriage and the Family,* 1975, *37,* 565–72.

Rosen, R. A. H. Occupational role innovators and sex role attitudes. *Journal of Medical Education,* 1974, *49,* 554–61.

Rosenfeld, C., and Perrella, V. Why women start and stop working: A study in mobility. *Monthly Labor Review,* 1965, *88,* 1077–82.

Ross, A. D. Some comments on the home roles of businesswomen in India, Australia and Canada. *Journal of Comparative Family Studies,* 1977, *8,* 327–40.

Rossi, A. S. Barriers to the career choice of engineering, medicine or science among American women. In J. A. Mattfeld and C. G. Van Aken, eds. *Women and the Scientific Profession.* Cambridge, Massachusetts: MIT Press, 1965.

———. Women in science: Why so few. In C. Safilios-Rothschild, ed. *Toward a Sociology of Women.* Lexington, Massachusetts: Xerox College Publishing, 1972.

Rossman, J., and Campbell D. Why college-trained mothers work. *Personnel and Guidance Journal,* 1965, *43,* 986–92.

Russo, N. F. The motherhood mandate. *Journal of Social Issues,* 1976, *32,* 143–53.

Ryscavage, P. More wives in the labor force have husbands with "above-average" incomes. *Monthly Labor Review,* 1979, *102*(6), 40–42.

Safilios-Rothschild, C. The influence of the wife's degree of work commitment upon some aspects of family organization and dynamics. *Journal of Marriage and the Family,* 1970, *32,* 681–91.

———. Towards the conceptualization and measurement of work commitment. *Human Relations,* 1971, *24,* 489–95.

———. Dual linkages between the occupational and family systems: A macrosociological analysis. *Signs,* 1976, *1*(3), 51–60.

Safilios-Rothschild, C., ed. *Toward a Sociology of Women.* Lexington, Massachusetts: Xerox College Publishing, 1972.

Salo, K. E. Women's views of their family and work roles. *JSAS Catalog of Selected Documents in Psychology,* 1977, *7* (Ms. No. 1518).

Sanville, J., and Shor, J. Leading ladies and gentlemen: Some clinical cues to transitional phases in husband-wife roles. *Clinical Social Work Journal,* 1973, *1*(2), 67–77.

Scanzoni, J. Sex roles, economic factors, and marital solidarity in black and white marriages. *Journal of Marriage and the Family,* 1975, *37,* 130–45.

Schaffer, H., and Emerson, P. The development of social attachments in infancy. *Monographs Social Research in Child Development,* 1964, *29* (3, Serial No. 94).

Scher, M., Benedek, E., Candy, A., Carey, K., Mules, J., and Sachs, B. Psychiatrist-wife-mother: Some aspects of role integration. *American Journal of Psychiatry,* 1976, *133,* 830–34.

Seiden, A. M. Overview: Research on the psychology of women, II. Women in families, work and psychotherapy. *The American Journal of Psychiatry,* 1976, *133,* 1111–23.

Shelton, P. B. Achievement motivation in professional women. (Doctoral dissertation, University of California, Berkeley, 1967). *Dissertation Abstracts International,* 1968, *28,* 4274A. (University Microfilms No. 68-5821).

Sieber, S. D. Toward a theory of role accumulation. *American Sociological Review,* 1974, *39,* 567–78.

Siegel, A. E., and Haas, M. B. The working mother: A review of research. *Child Development,* 1963, *34,* 513–42.

Simmons, J. Why do they want to stay home? *Cornell Journal of Social Relations,* 1970, *5,* 29–39.

Simpson, R. L., and Simpson, I. H. Occupational choice among career-oriented college women. *Marriage and Family Living,* 1961, *23,* 377–83.

Smith-Lovin, L., and Tickamyer, A. R. Nonrecursive models of labor force participation. Fertility behavior and sex role attitudes. *American Sociological Review,* 1978, *43,* 541–56.

Spelke, E., Zelazo, P., Kagan, J., and Kotelchuck, M. Father interaction and separation protest. *Developmental Psychology,* 1973, *9,* 83–90.

Sobol, M. Commitment to work. In Hoffman and Nye, eds. *Working mothers.* San Francisco: Jossey-Bass Publishers, 1974.

Spitz, R. A. Anaclitic depression: An inquiry into the genesis of psychiatric conditions in early childhood, II. *The Psychoanalytic Study of the Child,* 1946, *2,* 313–42.

Spreitzer, E., Snyder, E., and Larson, D. Age, marital status, and labor force participation as related to life satisfaction. *Sex Roles*, 1975, *1*, 235–47.

Stake, J. E. Women's self-estimates of competence and the resolution of the career/home conflict. *Journal of Vocational Behavior*, 1979, *14*, 33–42.

Standley, K., and Soule, B. Women in male-dominated professions: Contrasts in their personal and vocational histories. *Journal of Vocational Behavior*, 1974, *4*, 245–58.

Stein, A. H. The effects of maternal employment and educational attainment on the sex-typed attributes of college females. *Social Behavior and Personality*, 1973, *1*, 111–14.

Steinmann, A. Cultural values, female role expectancies and therapeutic goals: Research and interpretation. In V. Franks and V. Burtle, eds. *Women in Therapy: New Psychotherapies for a Changing Society*. New York: Brunner/Mazel, Inc., 1974.

———. Studies in male-female sex role identification. *Psychotherapy: Theory, Research and Practice*, 1975, *12*, 412–17.

Steinmann, A., and Fox, D. J. Attitudes toward women's family role among black and white undergraduates. *The Family Coordinator*, 1970, *19*, 363–68.

Stewart, A., and Winter, D. Self-definition and social definition in women. *Journal of Personality*, 1974, *42*, 238–59.

Sweet, J. A. *Women in the Labor Force*. New York: Seminar Press, 1973.

Tangri, S. S. Determinants of occupational role innovation among college women. *Journal of Social Issues*, 1972, *28*, 177–200.

Tatsuoka, M. M. *Discriminant Analysis: The Study of Group Differences*. Champaign, Illinois: Institute for Personality and Ability Testing, 1970.

Travis, C. B. Women's liberation among two samples of young women. *Psychology of Women Quarterly*, 1976, *1*, 189–99.

Trigg, L., and Perlman, D. Social influences on women's pursuit of a nontraditional career. *Psychology of Women Quarterly*, 1976, *1*, 138–50.

Turner, R. H. Some aspects of women's ambitions. *American Journal of Sociology*, 1964, *70*, 271–85.

U.S. Department of Commerce. *Marital and Family Characteristics of Workers: 1970–1978*. Special Labor Force Report #219.

U.S. Department of Commerce, Bureau of the Census. *Statistical Abstract of the U.S.*, Washington, D. C.: U.S. Government Printing Office, 1979.

U.S. Department of Labor. *Dictionary of Occupational Titles*. Washington, D.C.: U.S. Government Printing Office, 1977.

U.S. Department of Labor. *Occupational Outlook Handbook*. Washington, D. C.: U.S. Government Printing Office, 1978.

Van Dusen, R. A., and Sheldon, E. B. The changing status of American women: A life cycle perspective. *American Psychologist*, 1976, *31*, 106–16.

Vetter, L. Career counseling for women. *The Counseling Psychologist*, 1973, *4*, 54–67.

Vogel, S., Broverman, I., Broverman, D., Clarkson, F., and Rosenkrantz, P. Maternal employment and perception of sex roles among college students. *Developmental Psychology*, 1970, *3*, 384–91.

Wagman, M. Interests and values of career and homemaking oriented women. *Personnel and Guidance Journal*, 1966, *44*, 794–801.

Waldman, E. Children of working mothers, March 1974. *Monthly Labor Review*, 1975, *98*, 64–67.

Walker, L. S., and Walker, J. Factor analysis of students' attitudes toward working mothers. *Psychological Reports*, 1977, *41*, 723–27.

Walker, L., and Friedman, S. T. Professional women's attitudes toward the dual role of women. *Psychological Reports*, 1977, *41*, 327–34.

Ward, C. Is there a motive to avoid success in women? *Human Relations*, 1978, *31*, 1055–67.

Watley, D., and Kaplan, R. Career or marriage? Aspirations and achievements of able young women. *Journal of Vocational Behavior*, 1971, *1*, 29–43.

Weaver, C., and Holmes, S. A comparative study of the work satisfaction of females with full-time employment and full-time housekeeping. *Journal of Applied Psychology*, 1975, *60*, 117–18.

Weil, M. W. An analysis of the factors influencing married women's actual or planned work participation. *American Sociological Review*, 1961, *26*, 91–96.

Weinreich, H. What future for the female subject? Some implications of the women's movement for psychological research. *Human Relations*, 1977, *30*, 535–43.

Westervelt, E. M. A tide in the affairs of women: The psychological impact of feminism on educated women. *The Counseling Psychologist*, 1973, *4*, 3–26.

Wise, G., and Carter, D. C. A definition of the homemaker role by two generations of women. *Journal of Marriage and the Family*, 1965, *27*, 531–32.

Wolkon, K. A. Pioneer vs. traditional: Two distinct vocational patterns of college alumnae. *Journal of Vocational Behavior*, 1972, *2*, 275–82.

Wortis, R. P. The acceptance of the concept of the maternal role by behavioral scientists: Its effects on women. *American Journal of Orthopsychiatry*, 1971, *41*, 733–46.

Yockey, J. M. A model of contemporary feminine role change and family size. *Sex Roles*, 1975, *1*, 69–80.

_____. Role theory and the female sex role. *Sex Roles*, 1978, *4*, 917–27.

Yorburg, B., and Arafat, I. Current sex role conceptions and conflict. *Sex Roles*, 1975, *1*, 135–45.

Zambrana, R, Hurst, M., and Hite, R. The working mother in contemporary perspective: A review of the literature. *Pediatrics*, 1979, *64*, 862–70.

Zuckerman, D. Self-concept, family background and personal traits which predict the life goals and sex-role attitudes of technical college and university women. (Doctoral dissertation, The Ohio State University, 1977). *Dissertation Abstracts International*, 1978, *38*, 3923-3924B. (University Microfilms No. 7732016).

Zytowski, D. G. Toward a theory of career development for women. *Personnel and Guidance Journal*, 1969, *47*, 660–664.

Index

DiSabatino, M., 31
Dissatisfaction, and motivation for
    employment, 26-29
Dual-career families, 20-25
    family background, 38
    responsibility for childcare and housework
        in, 23, 85-86
    role conflict in, 21-24
    role conflict, differences between men and
        women in, 21-23
    time budget studies in, 22-23
Dual roles
    attitudes toward, 11-12, 13-14, 47, 82-85, 108
    attitudes toward, research groups, 56, 82-85,
        102, 104, 108
    child's age, influence on attitudes toward, 14,
        15, 16, 17-18
    coping mechanisms of women with, 24
    stress of, 21-23, 47

Education
    and career orientation, 63-64
    and female employment, 7-8
    research groups, 58, 63-64, 98-99
Employment, Female
    birth rate and, 4, 5, 6, 10
    changes in rates of, 3-6, 8, 46-47
    child's age and, 5-6
    and companionship type marriage, 37-38
    and demographic characteristics, 33-34
    education, effect on, 7-8
    family background, effect on, 33-35
    husband's income, effect on, 7, 28, 99
    husband's support, effect on, 31-32, 39, 107
    and incompatibility with motherhood, 10-
        12, 19, 29-30, 83, 95, 99-101, 102-103,
        108-109
    industrial development, effect on, 3-4, 9-10
    interruption, consequences of, 24-25
    motivations for, 26-29, 47-48, 98-100
    motivations for, research groups, 70-76, 89-
        92, 98-100, 104-106
    rates, married women, 4-5
    rates, with school-age children, 4-5
    rates, with pre-school age children, 6-8, 47
    social changes, affect on, 5-6
    See also Attitudes; Dual Roles
Eyde, L., 29, 35

Family background
    career orientation and, 40-42, 92
    and differences between working and
        nonworking women, 33-35
Family roles
    attitudes toward, research groups, 76-80, 82-
        85, 100, 102, 105, 108-109
    priority of, for women, 21-22
Farley, J., 17

Fear of success, 31
The Feminine Mystique (Friedan), 13
Financial Need
    and motivation for employment, 26-29, 99
    and motivation for employment, research
        groups, 70-74, 75, 76, 89, 92, 96, 99
Fox, D., 18
Frankel, D., 44
Frasch, C., 43
Freedom, motivation for homemaking, 30-31
Friedan, B., 13
Fuchs, R., 29
Fulfillment
    through motherhood, 11-12, 19, 20, 30-31,
        103
    and motivation for employment, 26-29
    and motivation for homemaking, 30-31, 103
    and motivation for plans, research groups,
        70, 74, 75, 91, 103-104
Full-time group, 49
    conflicts regarding plans, 69, 70, 87-89, 104-
        105
    educational level, females, 63-64, 104
    husband's support, 80-81, 105
    income, 64-65, 104
    motivations for plans, 70, 72-73, 74-75, 91,
        98-99, 104-105
    profile of, 104-106
    roles, expansion of, 78-80, 100, 105
    roles, importance of, 76-80, 105
    sex-role attitudes, 82-85, 92, 95, 100, 105
    sharing of responsibilities in, 85-88, 100, 105
    subgroups, 89-93, 105-106
    See also Research Groups

Garland, N., 18, 21, 23, 25, 58
Giffin, P., 56
Ginzberg, E., 35
Glenn, H., 14
Gordon, F., 49
Graef, R., 56
Grossman, F., 42
Gyllstrom, K., 22

Hall, D., 27, 49, 57
Hall, F., 27, 57
Hawley, M., 45
Heckman, N., 22, 23
Helson, R., 12
Hennig, M., 35
Herman, J., 22
Hewer, V., 14
Hite, R., 11, 12
Hjelle, L., 44
Hock, E., 30
Hoffman, L., 27, 28, 35, 37, 89
Home group, 49
    division of labor by gender, 86-89, 100